FUNDAMENTALS OF MARITAL THERAPY

BRUNNER/MAZEL
BASIC PRINCIPLES INTO PRACTICE SERIES

BRUNNER/MAZEL
BASIC PRINCIPLES INTO PRACTICE SERIES
VOLUME 14

FUNDAMENTALS OF MARITAL THERAPY

D. RUSSELL CRANE, Ph.D.

BRUNNER/MAZEL, *Publishers* • NEW YORK

Library of Congress Cataloging-in-Publication Data

Crane, D. Russell.
   Fundamentals of marital therapy / D. Russell Crane.
      p.   cm. — (Brunner/Mazel basic principles into practice
series ; v. 14)
   Includes bibliographical references and index.
   ISBN 0-87630-801-9 (pbk.)
   1. Marital psychotherapy. I. Title. II. Series.
RC488.5.C73 1996
616.89′156—dc20   96-34763
                                                  CIP

Published by
BRUNNER/MAZEL, INC.
19 Union Square West
New York, New York 10003

Manufactured in the United States of America
10 9 8 7 6 5 4 3 2 1

CONTENTS

PREFACE

This book introduces the basic ideas and principles of marital therapy. The emphasis is on methods that have a basis in the research literature related to couple therapy outcome and interaction. As such, it will emphasize methods that have been found to be important across several empirically tested models of treatment. The goal is to provide a basic understanding of marital therapy issues and provide a foundation for beginning work with couples and for additional study.

Many issues in the application of marital therapy have not been specifically addressed in the research literature. For these, some speculation grounded only in experience will be presented.

MARITAL VS. COUPLE THERAPY

Since the bulk of the research has been conducted using married couples, the book will emphasize treatment of married partners. However, many of the principles and ideas that have evolved from the study of married couples may apply to those who are not married but in serious and committed relationships. Consequently, the terms "marital therapy" and "couple therapy" may be used interchangeably, although the evidence that supports the use of these procedures with nonmarried partners is in its infancy.

HOW TO DO GENERAL MARITAL AND COUPLE THERAPY

The approach presented is designed to be general and practical. It will not deliberately concentrate on one model of treatment, nor is it intended to be a comprehensive review of the various models of treatment that are available. Instead, it will seek to outline basic issues, processes, and procedures that seem to be important for many forms of treatment.

INTERACTION VS. INTERPERSONAL PROCESS

The emphasis will be on the interaction of couples in the here and now of the therapy session. Instead of seeking to explore past unresolved conflicts or personal issues, it will focus on how to intervene in the interaction pattern that occurs between the partners.

LEVEL OF THE READER

This book is written for several groups of readers. First, it can be used as a text for upper division or graduate level courses in marital and family therapy. It can provide the basis for beginning work with couples with appropriate supervision.

Second, this text will be helpful to practicing professionals who wish to increase their skills in working with couples. For such readers, it can help provide a direction to understanding the dynamics of working with couples with an interactional perspective.

The concepts presented reflect the author's own experience and beliefs about treating couples. These include the beliefs that: (1) the partners should be worked with together whenever possible, (2) the interaction between the partners forms the unit of treatment, (3) the research literature should be used to understand couples and guide interventions, and (4) therapists are responsible for the progress of therapy.

ACKNOWLEDGMENTS

This book represents an accumulation of knowledge from and experience in my own research and clinical work with couples. Many of the ideas come from the research programs of others who have sought to learn to understand and treat couples in distress. Their efforts have built a firm foundation upon which others can contribute to and expand our understanding. I need not name them individually here; the reference list will acknowledge their individual and collective contributions to my thinking.

I would like to thank my friends and colleagues who have uniquely contributed to my knowledge and this project: Eugene Mead, for getting me started in scholarship and for the use of his splendid library, and William Griffin, who persuaded me to write this book.

I am personally indebted to Eileen Crane for inspiring this project and without whom it never would have been undertaken, or completed. Also to our children: Nathan, Keith, Ben, April, Michelle, Rachael, Sarah, and Scott for the joy they bring into my life and what they have taught me. I appreciate their sacrifices that make this work possible.

And to my students Quinn Bastian, Roy Bean, Jean Soderquist, and Trisha Weeks, for reading numerous drafts of the chapters and for their helpful and insightful comments.

Finally, to Shauna Pitts for her excellent help in the editing and organization of the manuscript.

FUNDAMENTALS OF
MARITAL THERAPY

1

WHY MARITAL THERAPY MATTERS: THE ECONOMIC AND SOCIAL CONSEQUENCES OF DIVORCE

Within the Western world social forces have combined to produce the highest divorce rates in history. The results of family disruption are devastating and have led directly or indirectly to many of the social problems faced throughout the world. Examples include increases in poverty for women and children, illegal drug use, gangs, and violent crime.

Divorce is not necessarily an outcome of unhappy marriages. Spouses can adapt to their situation in any number of ways. These may include physical separation, emotional withdrawal from one's partner, living with high degrees of emotional conflict, adopting a "business" marriage with few if any shared activities or interests, and simply deciding to live with a less than satisfactory relationship. Since these forms of adaption to unhappy relationships undoubtedly have their own consequences, marital therapy may serve such couples well.

On the other hand, divorce is a viable option for many couples. Since this is the case, a review of the research related to divorce seems to be in order. Consequently, the purpose of this chapter is to discuss several important issues related to marriage and divorce. Professionals who choose to work with couples in relationship therapy should be aware of the importance of their work. Familiarity with the consequences of separation and divorce may allow therapists to make a more sober appraisal of the importance of their work with couples.

This chapter is a summary and interpretation of the major research findings related to the consequences of family disruption. First, the economic issues associated with divorce and single-parent households will be addressed. Second, the findings of the major research projects on divorce outcomes will be reviewed. Finally, some possible implications for marital therapy will be presented.

Since most of the research has been focused on the effects of divorce on women and children, this review will necessarily reflect that perspective. Although the emotional consequences of divorce are undoubtedly no less severe for men, relatively little is known about their unique perspectives or circumstances. It is hoped that future researchers will address this important need.

WORLD TRENDS IN FAMILY DISRUPTION

Divorce rates are highest in the United States but are rapidly rising in many other Western countries. One model for explaining an increased divorce rate is economic in nature and proposes that increases in incidence of divorce are a natural consequence of the "full scale industrialization" of a country (Goode, 1992). Industrialization is said to generate the forces that make marriages unstable. These forces include (1) individuals' being less concerned with family role fulfillment, (2) development of a mass media that urges self-seeking, material advancement, and concern for self more than for the family as a whole, and (3) loss of respect for authority figures. All of these social forces seem to combine to produce greater marital instability and a general rise in the divorce rate (Goode, 1992).

Indeed, a major study of divorce trends, as associated with economic development, seems to support this notion. Clark (1990) examined the relationship between measures of socioeconomic development, individual economic dependency, religious affiliation, gender, age, and divorce rates. Economic data for 61 nations were available for analysis. The major findings were that (1) a higher level of socioeconomic development corresponds to a higher divorce rate, (2) societies in which women's roles as mothers and wives are valued highly have lower divorce rates, and (3) societies with greater participation by women in higher education and the job market have a higher divorce rate. This may be because less economic dependency on men enables women to seek divorce more frequently. If these predictors become more prevalent in more countries, one would expect to see worldwide increases in family disruption continue in direct relation to economic development.

In the United States, for example, Goode (1992) believes that two thirds of those married in the early 1990s can be expected to separate or divorce sometime in their lives. Evidence from other countries also suggests a similar increase in divorce rates. Studies by Goode (1992) and Maclean (1992) show significant increases in divorce rates for Australia, Austria, Belgium, England and Wales, Finland, France, Germany, the Netherlands, Japan, Norway, South Africa, and Sweden over the past 30 years. Even in countries where divorce is illegal (e.g., Republic of Ireland), the social processes that have driven others to divorce affect the citizens. Men and women separate, form new relationships, and set up other households with or without the legal action of divorce. The consequences of family disruption in these families are unknown, although one would expect them to be similar to the consequences in countries where divorce is permitted.

The social implications of the increased divorce rates have been described extensively by Goode (1992), who notes that the current divorce rates have no historical precedent except in times of great change, such as revolutions and civil wars, epidemics, famines, and conquests. These high divorce rates will continue to place a larger segment of the population in difficult social and economic circumstances for which the existing social institutions are not adequately prepared.

ECONOMIC CONSEQUENCES OF DIVORCE

Financial Support Costs for Single-Parent Families

One of the many reasons that the study of the economic consequences of divorce has become important is the large increase in the numbers of single-parent families. In addition, the large number of those who receive some sort of public assistance is a major concern. In the United States, public assistance is provided through the Aid to Families with Dependent Children (AFDC) program. AFDC legislation was enacted as part of the Social Security Act of 1935. Initially it was designed to provide for the needs of fatherless children, most of whom were expected to be orphans.

Currently, however, approximately 90% of families who receive AFDC support do so because their fathers are absent from the home because of divorce, separation, or the parents never having been married, and an important source of financial support is absent from the family. In 1988 the AFDC program had 3.7 million families and 7.3 million children enrolled. Widows and families with disabled fathers accounted for only 13% of these families.

If the past is any predictor of future trends, the numbers of families headed by nonmarried (divorced, never married, widowed, separated) women will continue to increase. In 1960 less than 7% of families were in this category; by 1985 this had increased to 21% of families. If present trends continue, 50% of children born in the 1980s will, at some time, live in nonmarried mother households before they reach 18 years of age (McLanahan, 1992).

In the estimated costs of the AFDC programs, one must include as well the cost of Medicaid, housing assistance, and food stamps, since AFDC recipients are also eligible for these programs. A recent estimate of the total cost of these programs was $24 billion in 1988 (Garfinkel, 1992).

In other countries, policies related to financial support vary, but the costs of such programs continue to mount. For example, in Australia most female heads of household receive their main income from social programs. The number of beneficiaries of these programs has tripled (in the decade 1978–1988), with a commensurate growth in costs (Funder, 1992). In the United Kingdom, more than 50% of female heads of household are on welfare; in Belgium the figure is 40% (Maclean, 1992).

Poverty Among Female Heads of Household

Many studies have found serious economic disruption for women and children following divorce. Men, on the other hand, often experience an increase in their standard of living. Consequently, the conclusion of most authors is that the burden of the economic costs of divorce is most often borne by women and children.

In the most comprehensive study to date, Finnie (1993) used data from Canadian tax records to track individuals before and after divorce. The study used a 10% random sample of the 1982 Canadian adult population that included 2,800 men and 3,075 women who were followed from 1982 to 1986. The conclusions were (1) the income of female heads of household dropped roughly one half and men's declined about one quarter in the first year of divorce, (2) poverty rates jumped for women in the first year, then dropped off slowly (but remained high), (3) over several years, women experienced steep declines in economic well-being while men enjoyed moderate increases, and (4) the gender earning gap and low levels of spousal/child support were considered to be the key factors underlying these patterns.

In another study, Laosa (1988) compared the annual incomes (including public assistance, alimony, and child support) of single-mother families and intact families across 20 different ethnic and racial groups in the United States. Without exception, the median income of the single-mother families with children under 18 was less than half that of intact families. In many cases it was one third.

Finally, in a recent review of the research on the economic impact of divorce, Sorenson (1992) noted that the economic consequences were worse for women than for men. This conclusion is very similar to that reported by Weitzman (1985). Her book reviewed the consequences of the "no fault" divorce laws. These laws have, in an attempt to make divorce less adversarial and to treat both spouses equally, led to a whole new set of problems due to unequal divisions of property and earning potential. As a result, many women with children find themselves in poverty following divorce. Decreases in income cause many children to live in poverty for an extended period. The greater the length of time in poverty, the greater the effects. Unfortunately, in the 1970s the average time in poverty was 4.6 years in two-parent and 7 years in single-parent families (McLanahan, 1992).

In a review of the literature regarding the multigenerational effects of divorce and poverty, McLanahan (1992) reports that children from mother-only families obtain fewer years of education, receive lower earnings as adults, and are more likely to (1) drop out of high school, (2) be poor, (3) receive welfare, (4) marry early, (5) have children early, both in and out of wedlock, (6) divorce, (7) commit delinquent acts, and (8) engage in drug and alcohol use.

These conclusions are similar to those in a study done in the United Kingdom. Maclean and Wadsworth (1988) reported the results of a long-term study of 5,000 children born in 1946. They concluded that those who experienced parental divorce showed inferior educational attainment and lower socioeconomic class than children whose parents did not divorce or those who had lost one parent through death.

When considering these results, one must use caution. It is difficult to separate the economic effects of divorce on children from the effects of other causes of single parenthood such as never married mothers or widowhood. Consequently, the effects attributable to poverty caused by divorce alone are not clear. However, McLanahan (1992) reported that studies that have made such comparisons have found similarities across all groups of families.

Spousal and Child Support

Spousal and child support does not protect children from poverty. This is caused by (1) inadequate amounts awarded by the courts, (2) reluctance of noncustodial parents to provide support, and (3) legal difficulties involved in enforcing spouse and child support payment orders.

In fact, some studies show that a surprisingly small number of divorced women with dependent children receive *any* support award (Finnie, 1993). Finnie (1993) reported that only 68% of Canadian divorces involving dependent children included cash awards. Of those, only two thirds of fathers paid support in the first year. The rates of payment dropped significantly thereafter.

In a study of American families, 114 ex-spouses were tracked over time. The results of this study showed the inequity between fathers and their children in terms of standard of living. The most common finding was that while the custodial mother was often poor, her ex-husband was usually not. In fact, the data show that ex-spouses were both poor in only 10% of the cases studied. Often, award amounts are so low that most fathers cannot truthfully claim inability to pay (Hill, 1992). The situation is similar in other countries. For example, in Belgium, child support awards are well below minimal estimates of the living expenses of children, and are paid infrequently (Maddens & van Houtte, 1992).

A remarriage by the custodial mother does not return families to the standard of living they enjoyed previously. One reason for this is that there is often a non-court-ordered decrease in child support payments when a mother remarries (Hill, 1992). When fathers remarry they often become responsible for additional children in their new family. As a result, fathers often have less money available to contribute to the support of their first family, even when their second wife is also working.

Welfare support is not sufficient to get women and children out of poverty. Most evidence shows that welfare programs in most countries were never intended to do more than provide a minimal level of assistance. For example, the Finnie (1993) study analyzed the effect of welfare payments on family poverty levels and found only a small effect on economic status from income generated by welfare payments.

Why Fathers Don't Provide Support

The reasons for nonsupport most often cited by fathers include (1) physical and emotional distance between father and child, (2) refusal by the custodial parent of visitation privileges, (3) the ex-wife's having sole custody, (4) negative relationship with ex-wife, and (5) a belief that the children do not directly benefit from the money they send.

Additionally, a father may be caught in the middle between his ex-spouse and children and his new spouse.

Marital tension in the new marriage in relation to children from former marriages may create barriers for fathers to continue to provide support. The potential for more children to be born to the remarried parent may also affect decisions about payments. Stepparents are often not willing to provide financial support to a nonresident child. In addition, supporting two families is often very difficult for families even when all of the parents are employed. They are then forced to make very stressful choices between children when the ability to support one family is difficult enough.

MAJOR FINDINGS ON THE CONSEQUENCES OF DIVORCE FOR CHILDREN

This section will present the result of two major research programs that have investigated the effects of family disruption on children. First, the developmental research program of Hetherington and her colleagues will be discussed. Second, the results of the California Children of Divorce Studies by Wallerstein and Kelly will be reviewed. Finally, some information about the effects of divorce on women will be presented.

Children's Vulnerability and Adjustment to Divorce

Hetherington has used a developmental psychology approach to study the effects of divorce, remarriage, and stepfamilies on children. The theoretical base has been the study of "vulnerability and protective factors" associated with children's adjustment to stress in general, and divorce and remarriage in particular. Most divorced spouses (about 75% of women and 88% of men) remarry. However, remarriages have a higher divorce rate than first marriages. Most of Hetherington's work has been based on the idea that divorce is not a single event but rather a "part of a series of transitions modifying the lives and development of children" (Hetherington, Stanley-Hagan, & Anderson, 1989, p. 303).

Some of her most important findings can be summarized as follows. First, during the first 2 or 3 years following a divorce, children in divorced families exhibit more externalized and internalized problems than children in nondivorced families (Hetherington, 1991). Externalized problems refer to antisocial, acting out behavior, aggression, and active noncompliance. Externalized problems interfere with the day-to-day interactions children have with their environment. Children with high rates of acting out behavior (e.g., hitting, stealing) have fewer friends, greater difficulty in school, and impaired relationships with their siblings and parents. It is common for acting out children to develop problems related to delinquency and violent behavior.

Internalized problems are passive behaviors such as dependency, anxiety, depression, and difficulties in academic endeavors and social relationships (Hetherington, Cox, & Cox, 1985). These behaviors are important because they can lead to clinical depression, excessive levels of anxiety, and social withdrawal. As a result, children may not be able to interact effectively with parents, teachers, or peers. Hetherington (1991) concluded that "children that undergo their parents' marital transitions are at greater risk for developing behavior problems than are children who remain in non-divorced families" (p. 346).

Repeated and multiple stressors that children experience during their parents' marital transitions may lead to externalized and internalized problem behaviors. For example, Rutter (1980) showed that a single stress typically carries little or no psychiatric risk for children. Yet, many children are exposed to multiple stressors in conjunction with their parents' marital transitions. These include (1) the marital conflict that contributed to the divorce, (2) the absence of the noncustodial parent, (3) a decrease in available financial resources, and (4) a lack of routine and family structure (Hetherington et al., 1989). In addition, the availability and efficacy of custodial parents may be extremely limited if they are working longer hours, going to school, or having a difficult time managing their own stress, depression, or disorientation (Hetherington, Cox, & Cox, 1982). As a result of these multiple stressors, children are more likely to have emotional and behavioral problems than children from intact families.

Following the initial 2- to 3-year period of adjustment to divorce, a child's success in adapting to and overcoming the differences inherent in the family situation is largely dependent on the complex interaction of several factors, including (1) gender (boys act out more frequently than girls), (2) age at which the divorce occurs (the younger the child at time of divorce, the better the adjustment), (3) gender of the custodial parent (children adapt better with a same-sex parent), (4) type and number of psychological resources available, and (5) the age of the child when the custodial parent's remarriage occurs (younger do better than older) (Hetherington et al., 1989).

The most important determinant of children's success in adjusting to the marital transitions is probably the quality of the custodial parent's adjustment to the divorce. Substance abuse, depression, and even accidents are more common among divorced than nondivorced adults (Hetherington et al., 1989). At a time when children are themselves confused and feeling a disorienting lack of structure, they encounter a struggling parent. It is fairly common, during this period of rapid and sometimes chaotic change, for parents to "make inappropriate emotional demands and elevate the older child to the level of a confidant" (Hetherington et al., 1989, p. 308). If excessive emotional and/or physical demands are made, the child may develop feelings of incompetence and resentment that could then lead to the child's expressing these feelings through inappropriate externalized and internalized behavior (Hetherington et al., 1982).

Single-Parent vs. Remarried Families

The adjustment to living in a one-parent family is usually much easier for children to make than is the transition to living in a remarried family. The externalized and internalized problems of the children are the same. When divorced parents remarry, however, this adjustment usually takes longer, especially for early adolescent girls (Hetherington, 1991). For example, Hetherington (1991) concludes that even 26 months after divorce, the majority of early adolescent girls with remarried mothers were still exhibiting more externalized problems than were girls with nondivorced parents or with a divorced but not remarried mother. Even though adolescence is usually a time in which such problems increase in daughters, a remarriage seems to make the adjustment of adolescent girls more difficult (Hetherington, 1972; Newcomer & Udry, 1987; Wallerstein, Corbin, & Lewis, 1988).

The findings of several studies, including Hetherington and colleagues (1982), are that children adapt better in single-parent and remarried families that are well functioning than they do in a conflict-ridden family of origin. Continued conflict, pre- or postdivorce, is detrimental to children, regardless of the family form. In other words, the more functional the current family, regardless of its form, the better the child does.

The most important point is that the difficulties that children experience may have more to do with the way their parents handle the marital transitions than with the divorce itself. When couples continue to generate high levels of conflict and acrimonious debate, their children suffer.

THE CALIFORNIA CHILDREN OF DIVORCE STUDIES

One of the leading research projects on divorce has been the California Children of Divorce study conducted by

Wallerstein and her colleagues. The study began in 1971 and followed 131 children and 60 families for more than 15 years (Wallerstein & Kelly, 1979). Through its longitudinal nature and clinical interview focus, this project has contributed in many significant ways to the understanding of how divorce affects families and children. In this project, there appear to be different responses to divorce depending on the age of the children at the time of the divorce. The four age groups that emerged were (1) preschool, ages 3–5, (2) early school-age, 5½–8, (3) later school-age, 8–11, and (4) adolescent, ages 12–18 (Wallerstein, 1986a, 1987–1988).

Effects on Preschool Children

Wallerstein and Kelly (1979) found that 80% of all preschool children in their study were "left almost entirely alone in coping with the confusing and terrifying departure of one parent" (p. 471). In contrast with some other studies, these authors concluded that at the end of 18 months, preschool children appeared to be "most vulnerable and susceptible to developing emotional and psychological problems" (p. 470) of all the age groups studied. Preschool children typically "regress" to an earlier developmental stage as one parent leaves the household (Wallerstein, 1986a). Intensified fears, sleep disturbances, and preoccupation with a fear of abandonment were most frequently reported. In addition, at 18 months after divorce, boys were significantly worse off than girls (Wallerstein, 1986a).

Effects on Early School-Age Children

Half of the 5- to 8-year-olds in her study suffered an abrupt decline in the quality of their school performance. Many children reported fear of being replaced in their families by another child. Wallerstein (1986a) reported that a typical response of boys was asking "Will my

daddy get a new dog, a new mommy, a new little boy?''
(p. 114).

At the onset of divorce, children ages 8 to 11 tended to
respond with anger toward one or both parents for causing the divorce. They suffered from grief, anxiety, loneliness, and a sense of humiliation from their own helplessness. Children in this age group tend to see one parent
as good and the other as bad. At least half suffer in both
peer relationships and school performance (Wallerstein,
1986a, 1987).

Children of divorce often suffer from what Wallerstein
classifies as the "overburdened child syndrome," which
can be characterized by two distinct factors (Wallerstein,
1986a). First, these children are often left alone for long
periods when they must care for themselves the majority
of the time. Work, such as cooking their own meals, doing
their own laundry, and taking care of their own basic
needs, is assigned to them. Second, the children may be
made responsible for the psychological functioning of one
or both parents. While inappropriate, parents may choose
to confide in children, who, consequently, lose their inno-
cence and are burdened with responsibility. These new
and difficult roles for children are complicated and unfa-
miliar. "They are not simple role reversals . . . because
the child's role becomes one of holding the parents together psychologically. It is more than a caretaking role"
(Wallerstein, 1987–1988, p. 110).

Effects on Adolescents

Children who are adolescents during a divorce often
show signs of moderate to acute depression, suicidal
thoughts, and acting out behaviors. Additionally, many
adolescents are preoccupied with worries of repeating
their parents' divorce (Wallerstein, 1985). These worries
may be manifest in an increased need for mental health
services. For example, Zill (1983) surveyed adolescents
who had experienced divorce before the age of 7 and

found that 30% of them had received psychiatric or psychological therapy by the time they reached adolescence. This contrasts with 10% in intact families. In another study, 5 years following the divorce, moderate to severe depression was found in one third of the entire adolescent sample (Wallerstein, 1991).

Wallerstein also found that 18 months following divorce, boys' psychological adjustment had deteriorated markedly, in contrast to a quick improvement in girls' psychological adjustment. Although young girls adapt to divorce earlier, they tend to have problems in adjusting later on (Wallerstein, 1986a). In a 10-year follow-up study on daughters of divorced parents, Wallerstein and Corbin's (1989) findings show "a distinct pathway for the girls, one characterized by the delayed emergence of powerful effects" (p. 602). At the 10-year follow-up, daughters who were ages 11 to 15 at the time of the divorce had recovered faster and were better adjusted than those who were older when the divorce occurred. At the end of 10 years, three fourths of those children 11 to 15 were well adjusted, compared to only 40% of those ages 16 to 18, and 27% of those from 19 to 23 at the time of the divorce.

Ten years following divorce, of those children who had reached the ages of 19 to 29, 68% had engaged in "mild to serious illegal activity during their adolescence or young adulthood" (p. 437). One third of the women had become pregnant out of marriage, and for 80% of them the divorce still held a moderate to high position in their psychological functioning. In interviews, several expressed that "divorce was better for them, but not for me; I lost my family" and "I lost the experience of growing up in a family unit" (Wallerstein, 1985, p. 440).

Overall, about half of the children showed acute behavioral changes demonstrated by an abrupt decline in "school performance, newly troubled peer relationships, and moody, irritable behavior" (Wallerstein & Kelly, 1979, p. 472). Most children recovered somewhat within a year. However, some of them developed chronic learning difficulties. Some adolescents began failing in their grades, demonstrating anxiety, intense anger, and depression (Wallerstein & Kelly, 1979).

Father–Daughter Interaction

It is also interesting to note that good father–daughter relationships were found only among the well-adjusted girls whereas poor father–daughter relationships were significantly associated with poor adjustment at 10 years. Wallerstein further points out that the attachment between mother and daughter, although beneficial in helping the development and adjustment of the daughter, can become a dilemma when the daughter's heterosexual relationships require that the dominant attachment with the mother be relinquished (Wallerstein & Corbin, 1989). Thus, that which was beneficial earlier may become a burden later.

Marital Conflict

One important factor in the children's reaction to divorce is the degree of conflict in their parents' marriage. In instances when parental discord is reduced, the reaction to divorce may be less distressed. However, if parental conflict continues after separation, children often display behavioral disturbances (Tschann, Johnston, Kline, & Wallerstein, 1990).

Reaction of Women

Wives in general do not do as well as husbands following divorce (Wallerstein, 1986b). Anger was found to be present in a significant number of females even 10 years after the separation. Over half of the women who divorced after the age of 34 continued to feel angry 10 years later compared to 15% who remained angry who divorced in their early twenties. There appears to be a difference in effects of divorce on women in relation to age. Women who were 40 years old or older at the time of the divorce are less likely to recover both socially and psychologically. In addition, in 40% of all women and 30% of all men, the sense of being rejected or exploited remained high after 10 years. Forty-seven percent of women and 46% of men had received psychotherapy and 50% of all women in the study remained clinically depressed.

STUDIES OF FAVORABLE OUTCOMES AFTER DIVORCE

Recently, some authors have criticized the work of Hetherington, Wallerstein, and others regarding the deleterious effects of divorce on children (e.g., Gately & Schwebel, 1992; Zuk, 1991). These authors find fault for two reasons: (1) the methodology of the earlier studies and (2) the use of clinical versus random samples of the population. Gately and Schwebel (1992) reviewed the literature on favorable outcomes of divorce and concluded that some children from divorced families seem to demonstrate "enhanced levels of functioning" (p. 57) in four areas: (1) maturity (children acting more mature for their ages than their nondivorced counterparts), (2) self-esteem, (3) empathy, and (4) androgyny.

In spite of the possibility that some children react positively to divorce, the overwhelming evidence is that for the majority of children, the consequences of divorce are far more negative than not. For example, a review of 92 studies comparing children in divorced single-parent families with children in intact families found that children of divorce scored lower across "a variety of outcome measures" (e.g., conduct problems, social adjustment, self concept) than did their counterparts from intact families (Amato & Keith, 1991).

EFFECTS OF UNHAPPY BUT STABLE MARRIAGES

Two studies (Amato & Booth, 1991; Booth & Edwards, 1989) have considered the effects of parental divorce and marital unhappiness on adult well-being. Findings from both studies are similar. In effect, they propose that remaining in an unhappy marriage has many more, and stronger, adverse effects on the next generation than parental divorce does by itself. They call for greater attention to be paid to the adverse effects of intact but unhappy homes.

Amato and Booth (1991) used longitudinal data to bolster their argument. They found that adult children of parents who divorced had lower levels of psychological, social, and marital well-being than those who grew up in intact, happy families. However, they were better off in those same areas than people who grew up in intact but unhappy homes.

CONCLUSIONS FROM THE RESEARCH LITERATURE

Children

The above studies of the effects of divorce on children conclude that there is an abundance of evidence for deleterious effects. This seems to be true for both lower- and middle-class children, but poverty greatly increases these negative effects. In fact, as previously discussed, the number of years a child lives in poverty is related to "nearly every negative outcomes measure devised" (Coleman & Ganong, 1992, p. 446). For middle- or upper-class children, the consequences remain severe, with identifiable impairments in emotional, behavioral, academic, and social functioning.

Mothers

For mothers, the economic consequences are similarly severe. Most women experience a significant decrease in their standard of living that results in poverty. For fathers, the economic consequences are less severe. This seems to be primarily the result of low levels of child and spousal support payments and the economic demands of remarried families.

Fathers

Very few studies have examined the consequences of divorce on fathers, although clinical experience suggests that it is a very difficult problem for them as well. Men typically report a great sense of loss and grief over being separated from their children, decreased self-esteem, stress associated with their financial obligations, and concerns about their ability to be involved in their children's lives.

POSSIBLE IMPLICATIONS FOR THERAPISTS

1. Marital therapy offers a potential way to help couples resolve their differences and prevent divorce. As such, it offers real hope to spouses who are embroiled in marital conflict. It is also a potential benefit for the children involved, since family conflict and disruption hurt children.

2. The effects of divorce and family disruption are borne primarily by children. As a result, therapists need to be aware of the likely outcomes for families who are facing this decision. Care should be exercised in making any recommendations about whether or not a couple should divorce or separate.

3. Those who are considering divorce should be fully aware of the likely outcomes for themselves and their children.

4. Mental health professionals should learn to do marital therapy as competently as possible to enable couples to have the best chance at rectifying their disagreements.

THE IMPACT ON INDIVIDUAL AND COMMUNITY

The purpose of this chapter was to show why marital therapy matters. In reviewing the research literature regarding the economic and social consequences of divorce, the following conclusions can be drawn

1. In the United States, divorce occurs in about one in two marriages. After a period of sharp increases, this rate has been fairly constant over the past few years.

2. Although the overall rate of divorce is lower in other Western countries than in the United States, the rapid increase in divorces is still apparent.

3. If present trends continue, at least 50% of children born in the 1980s will, at some time, live in non-married-mother households before they reach 18 years of age.

4. Divorce decreases the standard of living for women and children by as much as 50%. Men, on the other hand, do not suffer such large decreases. Their standard of living often increases over time.

5. This decrease in standard of living forces many women and their children into poverty. Children living in single-parent families are more likely to be poor themselves, as well as at risk for developing a number of behavioral and emotional problems.

6. Other problems associated with divorce include increased depression and anger in women and emotional and behavioral problems in children. Although little is known about the emotional and

psychological consequences of divorce for men, equally important and deleterious effects are likely.

Marital therapy is one way to help alleviate the consequences of divorce for men, women, and children. If couples can learn to resolve their differences, and decide to remain together, divorce may be prevented.

2

WHEN MARITAL THERAPY IS AND IS NOT APPROPRIATE

Marital therapy is a clinical, psychotherapeutic service to couples who are seeking to improve their relationship. It is characterized by treatment in which both spouses are present in the same session. The focus of treatment is on the couple's relationship, with increased attention to their current functioning. The emphasis is on the interaction patterns that occur between the partners rather than on the individual members of the dyad.

WHEN MARITAL THERAPY IS APPROPRIATE

Marital therapy is appropriate when the purpose of treatment is to improve the quality of a couple's relationship. There are several ways that couples present their request. First, the request for service comes in the form of relationship "enhancement." Couples in these cases request service as a way of improving their relationship. Typically, they will want to discuss ways to "understand each other more," learn to communicate better, or learn new skills to help them "solve problems better." In this kind of case the therapist would want to start with some sort of communication training to help the couple understand each other better.

The second request for service is from couples who see themselves as at risk for future problems, and who seek couple therapy as a way of preventing such problems from occurring. A typical example is couples who perceive their own backgrounds as dysfunctional and who feel inadequate regarding the task of developing a long-term relationship. Spouses might point to their own parents' failed marriages, a history of abuse or neglect in their families of origin, or a history of failed relationships of their own as reasons for seeking treatment.

In this situation the therapist might wish to assess the couples' current knowledge and skills in understanding one another. A good place to start would be to ask the couples what they consider to be their biggest areas of concern. After identifying the specific factors that they are worried about, therapy can then proceed around these issues. In some cases they are given educational materials such as readings and instructional tapes as an adjunct to therapy.

The third presentation will be a request for services from couples who see themselves as distressed and who are seeking assistance as a way to prevent worse problems from developing. These couples are concerned about their relationship. Although divorce or separation is not a current issue, they hope to prevent further deterioration in their relationship. In such cases, the process of identifying their current problems and concerns would be most helpful. Treatment can then be organized around those issues they are most concerned about, with a focus on the interaction between them.

The fourth presentation is couples who are clearly concerned about the possibility of divorce or separation. They typically want to discuss the possibility of separation or divorce and may see therapy as a last resort before such actions are taken. This group may include couples in which one partner has already made a decision to divorce or separate. In these cases, the appropriate action is to first discuss the possible alternatives. They may choose to pursue marital treatment, separation, or divorce. Ultimately, the focus of therapy will be determined by their own decisions. They may choose to attempt a reconciliation or, if necessary, pursue divorce mediation.

The fifth group includes couples who are close to divorce and seek therapy as a means of transition through the separation and divorce process. In this case, divorce mediation therapy may well be the treatment of choice, rather than couple therapy per se. The purpose of therapy in this situation would be to focus on the divorce process itself and the implications for the couple's future relationship. Issues may include division of personal and marital property, financial arrangements, tax considerations, and health insurance. In the cases where the couple has children, custody, support, and visitation arrangements need to be discussed.

Efforts to ameliorate the effects of the divorce on the lives of the children need to be made. In general, the consequences of divorce for children are worse when the couple continues to maintain a conflicted relationship. The focus of therapy now becomes more oriented toward protecting the interests of the children by attempting to make the divorce process as constructive as possible. Sometimes a truce can be developed to help protect the children from future harm. In other cases, couples may agree to separate but still maintain a focus on helping the children as much as possible.

The sixth group includes cases in which marital therapy is sought (or recommended) as an adjunctive procedure that follows or is concurrent with treatment of problems in another area. A typical example might be couples who, after seeking treatment for problems with a child, discover the importance of strengthening their own relationship as a necessary step in managing their child's behavior. Indeed, some studies have shown the usefulness of including a couple therapy component to the treatment of conduct disordered children (e.g., Dadds, Schwartz, & Sanders, 1987). In addition, some research suggests that marital therapy may be an appropriate treatment, either solely or in combination with other modalities, for such problems as depression in maritally distressed women, agoraphobia, and alcoholism (Alexander, Holtzworth-Munroe, & Jameson, 1994).

WHEN NOT TO DO MARITAL THERAPY

Marital therapy is usually not appropriate when the main presenting concern is an emphasis on "working on individual issues." In these cases, couples may request couple therapy but may really wish to receive individual therapy. The partners may well be involved in a supportive role, but the focus is not on the couple's relationship. Instead, the focus is on one partner, with the support and involvement of the other partner.

Couple therapy is also not appropriate when the couple (or a spouse) wishes to obtain a recommendation about the advisability of separation or divorce. In fact, providing such a recommendation would be unethical (American Association for Marriage and Family Therapy [AAMFT], 1991). In these cases, however, marital therapy may well be useful in helping the partners to explore options and clarify the ramifications both of divorce and of remaining together. Once the partners have made a decision, couple therapy to resolve differences or divorce mediation may proceed.

Couple therapy is also not appropriate when the goal of the couple is to separate or divorce. These couples should be provided with divorce mediation or divorce therapy. In cases where the goal of one spouse is separation or divorce, the appropriateness of beginning a course of marital therapy is questionable. Active participation by both partners is required for successful marital therapy. Both partners need to agree to the therapy action to be taken. A clear declaration of the intent of each partner may be the necessary first step.

Cases where physical violence is present are also not appropriately treated by couple therapy alone. Seeing the couple for marital treatment may result in increased stress and conflict and could increase the potential for further abuse. Couple therapy may be a very useful adjunct to other treatments designed specifically to handle domestic violence.

Couples in which one partner is chemically dependent are also not likely to be helped by couple therapy alone and should be referred for specialized chemical dependency treatment. Couple therapy may then follow successful intervention and treatment of the chemical dependency. Indeed, sobriety in a previously addicted spouse may lead to serious family and marital role strain as old patterns of behavior are changed. In these cases, the couple's therapy may focus, at least initially, on renegotiation of the couple's roles and rules of interaction.

If the case presents with severe psychopathology, the couple should probably not receive marital therapy alone. Although couple therapy may be helpful in some instances, the primary therapeutic task is not to work on the couple's relationship; instead, it is to manage and potentially resolve the psychopathology involved. Couple therapy can be helpful in working to manage the psychopathology or, as with chemical dependency, in renegotiating the couple's rules of interaction once the pathology has been treated.

In sum, marital or couple therapy is warranted for couples who are seeking to improve their relationship or who are concerned about the possibility of divorce or separation. It is also effective for couples who are considering divorce, but have not yet decided to separate. Marital therapy is not appropriate as the sole approach when chemical dependency, severe psychopathology, or physical violence is present.

3

COMPARATIVE APPROACHES TO MARITAL THERAPY

This chapter will review the three approaches to marital therapy that have received support in evaluation research: behavioral marital therapy, emotionally focused therapy, insight oriented marital therapy. A newer, research-based treatment, Minimal Marital Therapy, will also be presented. Focusing on the basic elements, or steps, of each model, this discussion will emphasize the elements that are common to all of the approaches.

BEHAVIORAL MARITAL THERAPY

Behavioral marital therapy (BMT) is the most extensively studied approach to couple therapy (Alexander et al., 1994). The effectiveness of this approach to treatment has been demonstrated on repeated occasions, with BMT being superior to no-treatment control conditions in every study to date (Jacobson & Addis, 1993).

The basic principles of this model were developed from social learning and behavior modification concepts in the early 1970s. Early authors focused on the use of behavioral exchange contracts between spouses, and communication and problem-solving training.

The behavior exchange process is the identification of specific behaviors to be increased or decreased and the establishment of agreements to facilitate these changes. The first applications of this procedure involved the development of formal contractlike agreements between spouses. These contracts were designed to target and change specific behaviors using specific rewards and penalties. For example, the wife may be asking the husband to spend more time with the family. His reward for so doing might be a special meal of his choice. His punishment might be having to pay a fine.

The communication and problem-solving components of therapy emphasize the development of new skills associated with learning to solve problems systematically. The first goal is to teach communication skills such as sending direct, short, and clear messages; listening by maintaining eye contact; and restating and reflecting the messages received. Next, the goal is to identify areas of disagreement, brainstorm alternative solutions, select alternative solutions, and write out an agreement that specifies who will do what, when it will be done, and how it will be done. Sometimes these agreements take the form of quid pro quo behavior exchanges where the appropriate behavior of one partner is reinforced by the other partner. Other times (especially in work with highly distressed couples) the contracts end up being agreements that are essentially between the therapist and each spouse.

The quid pro quo nature of behavior exchange agreements has led to mixed results. Some distressed couples react quite negatively to contract agreements. Consequently, an essential precursor to the implementation of any contract or behavior exchange agreement is the development of a collaborative set (Jacobson & Margolin, 1979). This concept refers to the couple's willingness to accept the therapist's definition of therapy (learning new skills) and comply with the therapy process, which requires role playing and practicing the communication, problem-solving, and behavior exchange skills that are to be taught in the sessions.

The results of the early contract and behavior exchange treatment approaches were mixed. Some couples improved with these approaches, but a significant group did not. As a result, a greater emphasis on the communication and problem-solving aspects of BMT was advocated. Recent research suggests that both aspects of BMT, behavior exchange and communication/problem solving, are essential for a long-term positive outcome (Jacobson & Addis, 1993).

An interesting addition to the BMT literature is the development of a cognitive-behavioral marital therapy (e.g., Baucom & Epstein, 1990; Beck, 1988). This model emphasizes the role of inaccurate or distorted assumptions and perceptions about oneself or one's partner. The focus is on changing these beliefs to create more accurate and realistic expectations about one's partner. The preliminary research regarding this approach is interesting, but it has not been shown to be very helpful with distressed couples (Alexander et al., 1994). These unimpressive results, however, may be attributed to the small sample sizes of the studies in question, or the relatively clumsy measures of cognitive processes currently available.

Historically, the focus of BMT has been on instrumental behaviors, with affection and emotional aspects of marriage receiving lesser emphasis. In response to approximately one third of the couples whose marital satisfaction did not improve substantially during the course of treatment (Jacobson, 1991c), the focus of BMT has been broadened to include cognitive and affective variables as well.

Recent BMT authors have moved well beyond the structured format of the early BMT technology to include many nonspecific treatment variables believed to be necessary for the successful application of BMT (e.g., Jacobson, 1991a). These nonspecific factors include such diverse techniques as "reframing" and "fostering emotional nurturance," both of which are not commonly associated with traditional BMT models of therapy.

These nonspecific factors (Jacobson & Margolin, 1979) are important in the delivery of clinically sensitive BMT. The focus of clinically sensitive BMT is on the delivery and implementation of therapy as opposed to the specific BMT technology itself. In some ways, it can be said that the focus of BMT has expanded to include a broader range of cognitive, affective, and emotional processes than previously emphasized. Indeed, one BMT author (Jacobson, 1991a) notes that "traditional BMT technology alone may not be necessary or sufficient for long-term change" (p. 142). Instead, the inclusion of insight, emotion, and the creation of intimacy seems to be important in almost any model of therapy (Alexander et al., 1994).

The question then may be raised as to what BMT is. For some (Johnson & Greenberg, 1991) BMT has been stretched beyond recognition. For others, BMT has simply returned to its functional analysis roots (Jacobson, 1991b).

In the end, it may well be that many of the treatment approaches currently under study produce similar results, by similar processes, but call these processes different names.

EMOTIONALLY FOCUSED THERAPY

Emotionally focused therapy (EFT) concentrates on "activating" powerful emotions and helping spouses to challenge their interpretation of their partners' behavior. The goal is to elicit powerful emotions in therapy and help couples challenge their own and their partners' dysfunctional cognitions about each other. It is based on the premise that attitudes and beliefs about one's partner reliably induce certain emotions and cognitions based on the assumptions or beliefs held. It is the *meaning* associated with the observation of one's partner's behavior that drives reactions. Thus, couples are brought to a high level of emotion, and the dysfunctional beliefs about themselves and their partners are directly challenged. It is through this process that couples learn more appropriate ways of thinking about themselves and their partner (Greenberg & Johnson, 1986).

The principal advocates of EFT describe four general principles in their approach (Greenberg & Johnson, 1988). First, while focusing on the *present* experience of each partner in the relationship, the therapist evokes recent problematic situations with the couple. In other words, using real issues, the therapist creates an environment where genuine emotions about these problems are reexperienced.

Second, as each partner experiences these strong emotions, the therapist focuses the couple on the issues of vulnerability and/or fears that are believed to underlie the couple's emotional processes. The couple is then encouraged to reveal these fears or feelings of vulnerability to each other, thus creating an atmosphere of genuine dialogue.

Third, the therapist helps the couple focus on how they fight rather than what they fight about. The specific problems presented by each spouse are important but are thought of as the "arena" where the underlying fears and vulnerabilities are manifest.

Fourth, the newly acquired genuine dialogue then becomes the vehicle for restructuring the interaction. The goal is to move away from the old defensive patterns into a different interaction style based on the couple's expressing their needs and wants in terms of their newly discovered primary emotions.

Implementation of EFT

Implementing this approach relies on nine steps:

Step 1: Delineate conflict issues in the struggle between the partners.

Both partners are encouraged to describe their view of the relationship and their concerns. The role of the therapist is to focus on the interaction between the partners rather than on the specific content being discussed. Ideally, the therapist "identifies and clarifies the positions each partner takes with the other, frames the problem in terms of emotional pain, deprivation of emotional needs, and secure attachment. . . . The focus is on the fears and vulnerabilities experienced by the partners in the relationship" (Greenberg & Johnson, 1988, p. 94).

Step 2: Identify the negative interaction cycle.

Therapists seek ways to elicit the repetitive negative interaction cycle that has been developed by the couple. The goal is for the therapist to see the cycle in action, then identify and describe it to the couple as it occurs in the session. In addition, the goal is to attempt to interrupt the negative cycle and substitute a more positive interaction pattern in its place.

Step 3: Access unacknowledged feelings underlying interactional positions.

The therapist then seeks to help the individuals access and accept their own unacknowledged feelings that underlie their actions toward their partner. The techniques are derived from Gestalt therapy and are used to identify emotions that are "central to the way the self is defined" (Greenberg & Johnson, 1988, p. 88). The goal is for both partners to "reprocess and crystalize their own experience in their relationship" (p. 89) so that each can then become emotionally accessible to the other. This is considered to be a key element of therapy, necessary but not sufficient for treatment success by itself.

Step 4: Redefining the problem(s) in terms of underlying feelings.

The next goal is to identify interaction patterns in order to help each partner understand the problem in terms of the underlying emotional needs that were identified in step 3. For example, a pattern of one partner's approaching the other while that partner withdraws can be recast as a problem of seeking assurance, with the other partner's feeling inadequate to meet the emotional needs of the approaching partner.

Step 5: Promote identification with disowned needs and aspects of self.

This step involves the reidentification of experiences in terms of their new labels and understandings. For example, the spouse who is approaching can learn to experience the feeling of seeking assurance in a different way, and the withdrawing spouse can interpret the emotional reaction of being inadequate or impinged upon in a more benign manner.

Step 6: Promote acceptance by each partner of the other partner's experience.

This step focuses on the validating of each partner's experience by the other. Two key events in this step are the identification and expression of the underlying feelings. In terms of acceptance, both partners must be willing to accept, believe, or trust that what their partner is describing is, in fact, true for them.

Step 7: Facilitate the expression of needs and wants to restructure the interaction.

Since the partners can now pursue a more open dialogue, the couple is led to express their needs and wants in more direct and honest ways. The idea is that once both partners can see their spouse in a more benign light (e.g., vulnerable instead of attacking), they are more likely to be empathetic and respond in ways that build trust.

Step 8: Establish the emergence of new solutions.

This step helps the couple reach new solutions to the problems that led them into therapy. Since they have learned to interact in more direct, less defensive, and more trusting ways, their discussions of problem areas are more likely to yield mutually agreeable solutions.

Step 9: Consolidate new positions.

Next, clearly identify the old and new ways of interacting. Then help the couple to articulate and describe each. This should help the couple to avoid returning to the old cycle as problems emerge. Rather, they will have a better understanding of both the old and the new styles and the consequences (both positive and negative) of each.

Research on EFT

Research regarding this approach has indicated some positive gains for couples in controlled outcome studies. Three outcome studies have been reported, and results for two of the three showed improvement for 71% of the couples (e.g., James, 1991; Johnson & Greenberg, 1985a, 1985b). However, it is interesting to note that, as was the case with behavioral marital therapy research, the group means reported for Dyadic Adjustment Scales (DAS) scores showed that in many instances, couples were still in the distressed range of less than 107 (couple mean) on the DAS marital quality measure (Crane, Allgood, Larson, & Griffin, 1990) immediately after therapy and again after 4-month and 1-year follow-ups.

INSIGHT-ORIENTED MARITAL THERAPY

The insight-oriented marital therapy (IOMT) model (although not yet readily available in the public literature) emphasizes a process of marital therapy that is primarily concerned with the "intrapersonal determinants of relationship distress" (Snyder, Wills, & Grady-Fletcher, 1991a, 1991b). As such, the focus is on unconscious feelings, beliefs, and expectations that are believed to be underlying the current marital problems.

The theory is that the unconscious processes, often rooted in early family-of-origin issues, are highly influential in the current marital problems. These unconscious processes can lead to such problems as "collusive interactions, incongruent expectations and maladaptive relationship rules" (Snyder et al., 1991a, p. 139). The goals are to increase both partners' understanding of themselves and each other, at a deep emotional level, and to work through emotional blocks to problem solving.

In this approach, therapists use a number of techniques such as "probes, clarification, and interpretation in uncovering and explicating those unconscious feelings, beliefs, and expectations" (Snyder et al., 1991a, p. 139). The idea is to break down emotional blocks and help both partners to address their own developmental issues that are interfering with their current relationship.

In addition, the therapist seeks to address these issues through intense in-session, here-and-now emotional experience of the couple. In this way, IOMT and EFT are similar in that both seek to heighten the intensity of the couple's emotional experience, and help them learn to experience this emotional arousal in different and more constructive ways.

Research on IOMT

Support for the efficacy of this approach comes from a 4-year follow-up study that compared IOMT to BMT with 59 couples (Snyder et al., 1991a). After 4 years, the IOMT couples had lower levels of deterioration of treatment gains and were less likely to have divorced than were the couples treated with BMT.

One difficulty in comparing the results of this study to other outcome studies is the use of dependent variables of marital quality that have not been used in other studies. This study used the Global Distress Scale of the Marital

Satisfaction Inventory (Snyder, 1981) as the main method of determining the distressed versus the happily married status of the couples. Because they used this idiosyncratic instrument, direct comparison of the couples used in this study with those in other studies of marital therapy outcome is impossible. Without the use of a common marital quality measure such as the DAS or MAT, the question of how severely distressed these couples were before and after treatment remains.

In addition, this study has been criticized by Jacobson (1991a) for its inaccurate representation of state-of-the-art BMT treatment. Jacobson contends that most of the procedures identified as IOMT techniques were considered "integral to a behavioral approach" (Jacobson, 1991a, p. 142). Although Snyder and colleagues (1991b) vigorously defend the treatment purity of their IOMT approach, confusion about just how different the various models of couple therapy are from one another remains. Another difficulty in understanding this model of therapy is the relative lack of a clear description of the approach. Almost all descriptions of the model are found in research reports that contain only skeletal sketches of it. As a result, the relative difference between IOMT and other models of therapy has yet to be described.

GOTTMAN'S "MINIMAL MARITAL THERAPY"

The minimal marital therapy (MMT) approach proposed by Gottman (1994a, 1994b) is based on a large body of marital interaction research related to the characteristics and interaction patterns of distressed and nondistressed couples. The conclusions of this research, collected for more than a decade, are that couples need to learn three important skills: (1) soothing , (2) nondefensive listening, and (3) validating. In addition, these skills need to be practiced to such an extent that they become almost "automatic" and can be used readily in times of high levels of emotional arousal.

Soothing is the ability to remain calm when confronted by a perceived threat. It can be described as either self-soothing or soothing of one's partner when the partner becomes angry or agitated. The therapist can provide soothing until the couples learn to sooth themselves and one another.

Specific self-soothing techniques include cognitive interventions designed to reinterpret the actions of one's partner. For example, statements to oneself such as "I know this is tough right now, but it will be all right" or "I don't have to take this personally" and other calming thoughts can be taught to spouses for use during conflict situations.

Spouse-soothing techniques include holding hands, maintaining eye contact, and whispering simple affectionate phrases. For example, whispering "I love you" or "This isn't going to drive us apart" might provide a good way to decrease negative interaction.

Gottman (1994a, 1994b) also suggests "stop action" techniques as a way to calm and sooth the couple. Examples include taking a break from the discussion or relaxation activities to enable the spouses to regain their composure.

Nondefensive listening is the ability to hear what is being said and to react in a neutral or positive way, without producing a defensive reaction such as denying responsibility, whining, complaining, or counterattacking.

Cognitive skills associated with this task are similar to the self-calming techniques described earlier. Rehearsing thoughts such as "This isn't personal" or "What I need to focus on is the ideas behind the scary words" may be helpful.

Another important skill in demonstrating listening is the use of simple eye contact and tracking gestures such as head nods, smiles, or saying "Uh huh" or "Yes, I see." The principle is that appearing to be paying attention to one's partner may be pivotal in demonstrating listening and in helping the couple not react defensively.

Validating means demonstrating that you are listening and that what is being said is being heard. It indicates that what is being said is important to the listener. Behaviors that can be validating include head nods, eye contact, relaxed breathing, occasional paraphrasing or restating of the speaker's comments, and brief vocalizations such as "Okay," "Yeah," or "I see." These comments demonstrate to the speaker that the listener is paying attention and understanding what is being said. It does not necessarily mean agreement, but it does demonstrate to the speaker that what is being said is important to the listener.

Research on MMT

There is as yet no evidence to support the efficacy of the MMT approach, but it does hold considerable promise. The three elements of the model are found in almost all other approaches to marital treatment and the model has been developed from some of the most sophisticated research methodology available.

Research Comparing Models

Several studies comparing different models of couple therapy have been done. A recent review (Hahlweg & Markman, 1988) examined four studies that compared BMT with other approaches. These authors concluded that there was little difference between the effectiveness of the approaches studied; this may be due to the increasing difficulty in separating out the unique elements from those found across all of the treatment approaches.

SUMMARY OF THE RESEARCH
ON MARITAL THERAPY

The literature is both "half full and half empty" regarding information about the effectiveness of the various approaches to couple therapy. In almost all cases where treatments have been tested and compared to a control group, the treatment has shown a reliable change (Alexander et al., 1994). But how much change has actually occurred? In most cases, couples improve from pretreatment conditions. Only about 50% of the couples treated by any method, however, are happily married at the end of therapy. Thus, all treatment approaches that have been investigated leave "substantial numbers of couples unchanged or still distressed by the end of therapy" (Jacobson & Addis, 1993, pp. 6–7).

The question also remains about how effective therapy is for couples who are seeking marital therapy but not volunteering to participate in a research project. These couples may be more typical of couples seen in therapy offices. They may certainly represent a different type of marriage than that of those who have been studied thus far. For example, one study of couples seeking therapy at a university mental health clinic (as opposed to those recruited for research on specific treatment) found somewhat better results in outcome (as measured by spouse self-reports). In the Crane, Griffin, and Hill (1986) study, 73% said they were improved, 20% reported no change, and 7% considered themselves worse off as the result of therapy. Consequently, for couples who are seeking treatment and receive a flexible and less "treatment manual" approach to therapy, the results are more encouraging.

COMMON ELEMENTS OF DIFFERENT MODELS

Given that the studies that attempt to determine significant differences between treatments have failed to do so, it may be helpful, instead of developing competitive theories, to examine the common elements of the different models and to devise an integrated approach to treating couples based on the research related to marital therapy outcome, marital interaction, and divorce prediction.

According to Alexander and colleagues (1994), the ingredients shown to be important in outcome include the following:

1. Affective changes (cognitive changes accompanied by strong affect)
2. Acceptance of unresolvable conflicts
3. Cognitive–emotional shifts and sharing of thoughts and feelings
4. Increased emotional engagement between spouses
5. Increased ability to manage and handle negative affect

In the chapters that follow, methods for implementing these key ingredients will be discussed. In addition, key research about marital interaction and therapy will be presented as a guide to the general procedures for treating distressed couple relationships.

4

WHY MARITAL DISTRESS DEVELOPS

The purpose of this chapter is to present an explanation for the development of marital distress that focuses on the role of attribution in the evolution of relationship problems. The principal idea is that in the early stages of their relationship, couples experience their partner in a very special (and positive) way. Similarities and differences are explored, and ideas and experiences shared. If positive interactions occur, friendship may develop, and shared emotional intimacy may follow. The process is artificially positive, however, since most dating and courtship interactions focus on shared pleasant events and activities. Couples spend time in recreation, in planned activities, and in spontaneous adventures. The amount of time spent in pleasant activities varies, but is usually difficult to sustain over a long-term relationship. The problem then becomes one of the degree to which the couple projects or anticipates this distorted level of positive interaction to continue into the future. If they expect the future to be quite similar to their dating experience, they are likely to be disappointed since the level of activity in which they were previously engaged becomes more and more difficult to maintain.

The experiences of such a limited range of behavior over a relatively brief period can lead to some serious misconceptions about what the future may entail. If the couple's expectations are not realistic, disappointment may occur and resentment of one's partner may begin to develop.

In addition, there may be a tendency to maximize similarities and minimize differences as the relationship progresses. The tendency is to see the positive and pleasant things about one's potential partner and not see or minimize the annoying or disagreeable characteristics, habits, or behaviors. This "filtering" process leads to expectations that can be unrealistic at times. For example, in early dating, couples may become enthralled by their partner's appearance, charm, or generous nature. As they get to know each other better, however, the initial attraction may be replaced by a more realistic appraisal.

Dating and early stages of relationship development, then, can be seen as producing an emotional atmosphere that is quite different from that found in later stages of the relationship. In dating there is often a focus on positive interactions, with a tendency toward overlooking or minimizing negative experiences with the other. These initial positive experiences may be followed by an often unrealistic set of expectations about how this extreme "high" will be maintained or even heightened over time.

Unfortunately, the honeymoon phase ends and the everyday tasks of life and relationship development begin to be salient to the partners. What then? If couples are prepared to expect a difference in the relationship over time, they are more likely to appreciate their partner and be willing to work to maintain and enhance their relationship. On the other hand, if they start to notice differences between their past and present situation and then begin to blame their partner for their own disappointments, they could very well launch an escalating negative cycle.

Blaming one's partner for problems can lead to a change in attitude and a change in behavior toward the partner. These changes are seldom positive. Instead, they emphasize the differences between partners, or perceived inadequacies and weaknesses in one's partner. Although it is unlikely that most long-term relationships will be devoid of disappointments or that annoying behavior won't become more apparent for many partners, what spouses do about these disappointments and differences is crucial. Those who accept such disappointments and differences as an inevitable part of life and who can focus on developing the positive similarities seem to do better in the long run. On the other hand, partners who notice the differences and disappointments and then begin to criticize and blame their partners usually do not do well.

Why? It may be because one partner's deciding there is something wrong with the other and, more important, that he or she, as spouse, can "fix" the other, will often lead to a number of excessive attempts at behavior change. These attempts may take the form of, first, persuasion, then complaining, then criticism, then criticism of the other partner to others, and finally threats. Though these behaviors are designed to try to influence the behavior of the other partner, many partners consider such behavior to be at the least unpleasant and, more likely, demanding or controlling. The typical responses to such behavior change techniques are quiet acquiescence, passive aggressive reactions, active refusal, and, most often, active retaliation with criticisms, sarcasm, complaints, and threats of one's own. As the two spouses interact, both attempting to change the other's behavior, they end up working together to create a negative interaction cycle. This negative cycle then replicates itself over time, often becoming stronger with each cycle of punishment/counterpunishment, until the spouses become adversaries.

As adversaries, couples then become concerned with justice, who is to blame, and retaliation for perceived injustices. This emphasis on negative outcome, expectations of negative interactions, and a willingness to reciprocate perceived or real offenses can then dominate the day-to-day interactions for couples. Indeed, such negative interaction cycles are highly characteristic of distressed couples (see Chapter 11).

The central issue at this point becomes "acceptance or nonacceptance" of one's partner. Those who basically accept each other do better; those who do not, don't. This does not imply a blind acceptance of everything a partner does. There is conflict in every relationship just as there are compromises that need to be made and skills to be learned to make understanding and compromise more likely. Rather, an attitude of basically accepting and respecting one's partner seems to be necessary for long-term relationship satisfaction and stability.

WHO DECIDES WHAT DIFFERENCES SHOULD AND SHOULD NOT BE ACCEPTED?

In any discussion about accepting differences, the question about what differences are, or should be, acceptable comes to mind. The first question is often "Who decides which differences should not be accepted?" It is important to assess whether the expectation is based on a person's sincere personal concern or on the concerns of others such as friends or family members. Some spouses are led to expectations about their relationship because of the expectations of others. In these cases, the difference between spouses is someone else's issue, enacted through one spouse. Ultimately, spouses must decide for themselves when any difference is too large to accept, if it should be discussed, or if some negotiation is required. However, there are several ideas that may be useful in helping spouses decide which are the very important issues to them.

First, is the issue consistently important in day-to-day interaction? Examples include differences in personal hygiene, child-rearing practices, money, family and friends, and work. The more consistently a difference becomes evident, the more important it becomes as a topic for discussion and possible negotiation. On the other hand, is it an issue that occurs infrequently? Such differences that need to be handled on an infrequent basis are good candidates to ignore.

Second, are the effects of the difference very powerful? If so, the difference needs to be resolved because it can have dramatic and negative effects. Many times, the difference can be very painful for one partner. Examples include battering, gambling, excessive alcohol or drug use, and uncontrolled credit purchases. Since real harm is possible, issues such as these need to be addressed directly.

Third, are the differences offensive to the values or beliefs of one partner? In these cases one partner may consider a difference to be relatively unimportant, while the other partner considers it to be vital. Examples include alcohol or drug use in the perception of teetotalers, physical punishment of children, strong expectations about gender roles, proper conduct, faithfulness, and honesty. In these cases, the partner with the greatest concern should be acknowledged and the issue addressed. The personal values of the therapist are not critical in deciding whether or not an issue is important. If one spouse believes it is important, then it *is* important.

THE BIG THREE: PROBLEMS OF POWER, TRUST, AND INTIMACY

Regardless of how the particular problems in a relationship develop, there are three themes that often may be used to analyze the "issue behind the issue." These issues include power (who has it, in what proportion, and how it is used), trust (how and whom to trust), and intimacy (emotional and sexual).

Power refers to the relative dominance of one partner over the other. Some couples have relatively structured relationships where one partner is clearly the most dominant. Others structure their relationship in terms of competence. That is, whoever is most competent in an area is responsible for that area. Others divide power into separate domains based on traditional sex-role organization. Still others desire a more egalitarian approach and seek to divide power equally between them.

Some good questions to ask that may lead to ideas about the balance of power in a relationship are: When the chips are down, who decides? How was it decided who is to decide? Who criticizes whom? Who speaks for whom?

Trust refers to the ability of individuals to depend on their partners to keep confidences, respect vulnerabilities, maintain commitments, honor agreements, and so forth. Trust is an important ingredient for marriage because it provides a basis for understanding and predicting the future. If spouses trust one another, they are able to anticipate their partner's behavior in the future. The ability to predict what one's partner will do in a given circumstance allows a sense of emotional security in the relationship.

Some partners come to marriage with an impaired ability to trust deeply. Persons who have experienced a number of deep disappointments in intimate relationships are especially likely to have trouble in this area. Examples include those raised in alcoholic families, victims of abuse, and those whose own parents had difficult marriages. Those who have trouble trusting others will have difficulty trusting their partner. This lack of trust can manifest itself in problems related to emotional expression, intimacy, and control issues.

Intimacy refers to emotional and psychological closeness often associated with the ability and willingness to express feelings and share experiences and emotions. Intimacy is important because the level of intimacy that one experiences in relation to one's partner is often predictive of marital satisfaction (e.g., Harper & Elliott, 1988). Also, lack of intimacy is often identified as a problem by couples seeking marital therapy.

Emotional intimacy is often associated with sexual intimacy, but the two are distinct constructs. Emotional intimacy refers to sharing thoughts and feelings and for many couples is often an essential precursor to sexual intimacy.

How Problems of Power, Trust, and Intimacy Are Manifest

These three basic issues of relationships frequently overlap and often yield similar presenting problems. These usually include concerns about sex, money, and communication. Why these three presenting problems? Primarily because they are relevant and important in the day-to-day interactions of most couples. They are also issues that are particularly vulnerable to the effects of mistrust, dishonesty, and lack of understanding between partners.

Sexual issues, in particular, are sources of conflict because successful sexual adjustment usually requires, as a prerequisite, a degree of trust, honesty, intimacy, and emotional commitment. When these conditions are not met, spouses often present with concerns about sexual matters.

If the sexual issue is driven by power, trust, or intimacy problems, the presenting sexual problems are most frequently complaints about infrequent sex, uncomfortable or painful intercourse, and orgasmic problems. Sex becomes infrequent when one or both partners have trouble in giving themselves to the other at a deep emotional level; it can be uncomfortable because a satisfactory level of arousal is not achieved before intercourse. In both cases, the underlying issue is probably fear of being hurt again by whatever has led to the mistrust and lack of intimacy that currently exists.

Problems regarding money are often associated with issues of power and trust, but less with intimacy. Power is a factor because one or both partners may wish to exert their domination over the other by keeping all of the family money or controlling how the resources of the family are used. Another variant of the power theme in finances occurs when one or both partners assert their "independence" by refusing to answer questions regarding money—how it is spent and for what reasons. Such couples may develop a "yours versus mine" approach to their family finances when a cooperative strategy would be more helpful in the long run.

Couples who have difficulty trusting one another may also have difficulties in handling their family finances. These couples demonstrate a "stingy" approach to money, safely guarding their own assets and demonstrating an unwillingness to share what they have accumulated. The overriding concern may be that for some, money represents a degree of power and safety. The pursuit of financial security may be more important than allowing both partners to participate in controlling their own (and their family's) financial future.

Problems regarding communication are also associated with power, trust, and intimacy. Power problems appear when one or both partners wish to dominate conversations in order to compel or convince their partner of the folly of their ways or to justify their own opinion. Another tactic is to attempt to force an agreement or stop a discussion by the sheer weight of the rhetoric presented. Typically this includes such behavior as interrupting, talking over one's partner, and demonstrating disgust or ridiculing one's partner's ideas or opinions.

Lack of trust and difficulties in intimacy yield problems in communication such as halting discussions, unwillingness to express opinions (either in silence, "not knowing," or not having any concerns), low levels of personal disclosure, and unwillingness to discuss matters that are emotionally sensitive.

Other Manifestations of Problems of Power, Trust, and Intimacy

Problems in these areas also may lead to feelings of loneliness, and isolation. When one partner's attempts at developing a close relationship are rebuffed, this can lead to feelings of discouragement about trying to maintain a level of commitment to and concern about the other partner. In some cases, this may also lead to an emotional withdrawal from the other partner. The absence of emotional support and a satisfactory level of intimacy may, in turn, lead to a lonely and sometimes desperate existence. In such cases, spouses may look elsewhere (e.g. friends and family) for emotional support. They may develop strong emotional attachments to family and friends who may begin to take the place of a spouse in terms of emotional security and support. In certain situations, this level of emotional involvement may lead to emotional or sexual extramarital affairs as well. Many cases of extramarital involvement can be traced to a search for emotional support and encouragement.

HOW DIFFERENCES IN GENDER-ROLE EXPECTATIONS CAN LEAD TO THE DEVELOPMENT OF MARITAL CONFLICT

One additional source of conflict in relationships is the ways in which the partners enact their beliefs and expectations about what is appropriate and inappropriate gender-role behavior. Gender roles are the implicit and explicit assumptions spouses make about what are the correct, proper, or right ways they are supposed to act in their role as husband or wife (or mate) in a relationship. Relevant issues are work and career responsibilities, the division (or lack of division) of household labor, child care, initiating sexual relations, and so forth.

Couples vary on these issues, ranging from highly traditional to very egalitarian in their expectations. There does not appear to be any form of relationship that is most advantageous, but *agreement* about what is expected seems to be the most critical factor in how couples handle these issues.

CONFLICTS RELATED TO VALUES

Values can also lead to conflict when partners have very different ideas about what is good and desirable conduct related to important issues in their lives. Matters such as expectations about gender roles, relationships with family and friends, religion, conventionality, and other philosophy-of-life considerations are also potential sources of marital conflict.

5

WHAT WE KNOW FROM THE RESEARCH ABOUT COUPLE THERAPY

The purposes of this chapter are: (1) to review what is known about treatment outcome of couple therapy; (2) to discuss some of the behavior patterns that distinguish distressed from nondistressed couples; and (3) to discuss potential issues related to couple therapy outcome that have yet to be studied in detail.

SUMMARY OF TREATMENT OUTCOME STUDIES

The history of marital therapy research is dotted with articles that review the many treatment outcome studies on couple therapy (e.g., Alexander et al., 1994; Baucom & Hoffman, 1986; Gurman, Kniskern, & Pinsof, 1986; Hahlweg & Markman, 1988; Jacobson & Addis, 1993). This chapter will not attempt to replicate these efforts. Rather, it will summarize these reviews into a set of statements regarding what is known about treating couples.

First, all studies of treatment outcome show that treatment is better than no treatment for increasing couples' marital satisfaction.

Second, a substantial number of couples improve but remain distressed after treatment is concluded. However, over 70% of couples report improvement in their relationships as a result of therapy (Crane et al., 1986).

Third, differences between treatment approaches are hard to evaluate since many share similar features. Many comparative studies have failed to show important differences between the various approaches to treatment. Also, when differences are found they tend to be in the direction of the theoretical model favored by the primary investigators.

Fourth, most research has been done on moderately distressed couples. Consequently, it is not known how well more severely distressed couples respond to treatment. The average Marital Adjustment Test (MAT) score for couples participating in therapy research projects is about 82 (Hahlweg & Markman, 1988). These couples are most accurately described as moderately distressed, defined as within one standard deviation of couples who are normally represented in therapy research studies (Crane et al., 1990).

Fifth, most research on treatment modalities has focused on younger couples. For example, the average age of couples seen in research treatment programs is about 32 years (SD = 3.4) (Hahlweg & Markman, 1988). Little is known about treating older couples.

Sixth, couples who are more traditional in their sex-role orientation may be less likely to benefit from BMT (Jacobson, Follette, & Pagel, 1986). The same may also be true of couples treated with EFT since couples must "wish to reorganize their relationship in terms of an intimate partnership" (Greenberg & Johnson, 1988, p. 59). The goal of an intimate partnership may not be appropriate in some cases.

The assumption of an egalitarian relationship may be a problem for more traditional couples. Traditional couples may not wish to accept egalitarianism as an appropriate structure for their relationship. Such couples generally quickly discontinue therapy when faced with such a conflict.

Seventh, couples who are emotionally disengaged from each other are less likely to benefit from treatment (Hahlweg, Schindler, Revenstorf, & Brengelmann, 1984). They may well be those who are in the midst of a psychological divorce and are now just beginning the physical and legal divorce process.

CHARACTERISTICS OF DISTRESSED AND NONDISTRESSED COUPLES

The purpose of this section is to describe the common characteristics that distinguish distressed from nondistressed married couples. The goal is to provide a background to understand what one can expect in working with distressed couples. In other words, one can anticipate that individual partners in distressed relationships will act quite differently toward each other than will partners in nondistressed relationships. Understanding these differences will allow a therapist to identify which couples are more severely distressed and therefore to focus on problems commonly found in distressed couples.

In general, the following conclusions seem to hold across a number of studies and for a number of populations (Gottman, 1994a; Schaap, 1984). Findings from laboratory investigations will be presented first as they are more likely to reflect couples' in-session behavior.

First, distressed couples are predominately negative in their verbal interaction and attitudes. This is evident in emotional expression, communication, and problem-solving attempts, even with low-conflict situations. Specifically, distressed couples show more negative affect, coercive acts, negative social reinforcement, and defensive behaviors. They also speak more loudly and maintain greater interpersonal distance from their partner. In contrast, nondistressed couples show more positive affect, social reinforcement of each other, reconciling acts, and facilitating and supportive behavior while keeping less interpersonal distance (Crane, Dollahite, Griffin, & Taylor, 1987; Crane & Griffin, 1983).

Second, conflict resolution is much more difficult for distressed couples. They are more likely to emit negative and coercive behavior toward their partner. In addition, conflict is longer and more intense in distressed couples. Apparently, they have little ability or inclination to exit conflict cycles. Nondistressed couples, on the other hand, are more likely to ask more questions, be less demanding, and use fewer personal attacks than are their distressed counterparts.

Third, the principle of reciprocity operates differently for distressed than for nondistressed couples. For distressed couples, reciprocity is primarily associated with negative exchanges and punishing behaviors that are delivered quickly. For nondistressed couples, reciprocity is associated more with positive exchanges that can occur over much longer periods. When good things happen between the spouses, they are more likely to reciprocate with positive behaviors, but the exchange may occur at a later time.

These laboratory results have been summarized by Gottman (1994b) into five main behavior clusters that distinguish distressed from nondistressed couples. The first characteristic is *criticism*. Criticism is an attack on the other person's character or personality. There is usually a great deal of blame associated with the attack, and it is personal, not just a complaint about a problem situation or behavior. Blaming one partner for a problem or attributing the problem to the spouse's bad intent or personality deficits is routinely done in these criticisms. For example, one spouse might say "You didn't pick up the laundry because you only think of yourself."

The second behavioral cluster is *contempt*. Contempt is similar to criticism, but it adds to the attack the element of "intent to insult and psychologically abuse" (Gottman, 1994b, p. 79). Typical contemptuous behaviors are insults and name-calling, mocking, hostile humor (contempt covered by a thin layer of humor), and certain body language such as sneering and rolling eyes.

The essential difference between criticism and contempt is that criticism is a personal attack, whereas contempt is an escalation of the criticism to include the devaluing of one's partner. For example, one spouse might say "You didn't pick up the laundry because you only think of yourself . . . you are lazy." Here, the presence of a personal devaluing differentiates criticism from contempt.

The third behavioral cluster is described as *defensiveness*. Defensiveness is highly disruptive to communication of all kinds, including affectionate interchanges and conflict resolution. The presence of defensiveness in a relationship relies on the couple's mutual perception of having been wronged by the other partner in some way. They often express righteous indignation about something that has been done, or they may describe themselves as victims of their spouse's actions.

Defensiveness is reflected in poor communication and problem-solving skills. Examples include denying responsibility, making excuses, cross-complaining (as in "What about what you did?"), yes-butting (for example, one spouse might say "I know you have a point about going to school, but I can't go if you don't support me"), repeating, whining, and negative body language such as a false smile or folding one's arms across one's chest.

Stonewalling describes the fourth cluster. An essential feature here is that spouses stop responding to critical, contempt-laden messages. Instead, they habitually ignore what is being said and remove themselves, at least emotionally, from the situation. Stonewalling (most frequently by husbands) usually leads to increased frustration and escalations of attacks from the engaging partner (most often wives), thus fueling increased stonewalling and disengaging behavior by the withdrawing spouse.

The final cluster involves high levels of *ruminating on negative, distress-maintaining thoughts*. How spouses think about their partners determines a great deal of how they treat them. For distressed couples, these thoughts include being an innocent victim, or feeling righteous indignation about what has been done. In addition, thoughts that maintain contempt and give partners the evidence they need to treat each other contemptuously occur frequently. Some additional examples include remembering each perceived injustice, labeling one's partner in a contemptuous way, and thinking about all of the problems that have occurred over the years. These can all contribute to a high level of emotional arousal, producing criticism and punishing exchanges.

Through the processes of criticism, contempt, defensiveness, stonewalling, and ruminating, couples often develop an increasingly negative and escalating coercive interaction pattern. Each cluster of behaviors fuels the others as partners gradually are pulled apart.

CONCLUSIONS

Couples Who Respond Well to Therapy

Couples that seem to respond well to therapy (at least the way marital therapy is conducted in university treatment research programs) are relatively young, Caucasian, educated, moderately distressed, in first marriages of relatively short duration, and from the middle classes (Alexander et al., 1994). These types of couples will most often report significant improvements in their relationship as a result of treatment, however, some will not improve. The problem is how to distinguish those couples that are likely to benefit from therapy from those who are not. In addition, there are a number of variables that are associated with marital adjustment and stability that may be important in working with couples. The influence of these variables on the delivery of marital therapy has yet to be understood.

Variables That May Affect Therapy

Little is known about a range of variables that are recognized to influence marital quality and stability and are therefore likely to affect the progress of marital therapy as well. These include marital status (cohabiting couples vs. those legally married), high or low social class, ethnicity, gender differences in responsiveness to therapy, couples in second or subsequent marriages, similar versus dissimilar values and belief systems (such as religious orientation), and a variety of other issues (Larson & Holman, 1994).

Several researchers suggest that *cohabiting* couples are less committed to the institution of marriage, may be more unconventional, and are less concerned about the stigma of divorce (e.g., Thomson & Colella, 1992; White, 1990). Those who cohabit may be together for reasons quite different from the reasons of those who have married. For some, cohabitation is a form of trial marriage where partners are evaluated for mutual compatibility. For others, it is a convenient way to obtain intimacy without making a long-term commitment (Cherlin, 1992).

Because couples who are cohabiting are not well represented in the research studies to date, this information suggests that couples who are currently cohabiting may need a different approach to treatment than those who are married.

There is considerable evidence (Cherlin, 1992; Larson & Holman, 1994), however, that couples who marry after living together have generally poorer marital adjustment and stability after marriage than those who did not live together. Still, little is known about the unique processes at work for such couples. One possibility for treatment, however, might be to discuss the issue of commitment very early on. This does not mean discussing legal marriage; rather, it means trying to identify the rules that the couple have accepted for maintaining or ending their relationship. One might ask, "Under what conditions are you willing or unwilling to continue your relationship?" The questions asked are similar to those asked of married couples, but commitment, in particular, may be an important issue for these couples.

As noted by most research reviews, the couples most often seen in therapy research come from the middle class. Little is known about what works with the couples located on either side of the middle on the *economic/social class* continuum. Some research has shown that the higher levels of education and income of affluent couples are helpful in facilitating marital adjustment in the future (Larson & Holman, 1994). Thus, one could anticipate the need to design treatment related to social class. More affluent (and more educated) couples may be more likely to respond to experiential or intellectually based treatment. On the other hand, less affluent (and less educated) couples may need a more directive approach.

The influence of *ethnicity* on the effectiveness of marital therapy is also poorly understood since very few ethnic minority couples have been represented in therapy research (Bean & Crane, 1996). Some research (Oggins, Veroff, & Leber, 1993) suggests there may be more affective intensity in African-American marriages than in Caucasian couples. As a result, treatment interventions that focus on direct interaction may be most helpful with members of this group.

Gender differences in responsiveness to therapy are likely to occur since the determinants of marital satisfaction seem to be different for men and women (Larson & Holman, 1994). One study (Allgood & Crane, 1991) showed that husbands' anxiety was predictive of dropout in couple therapy, suggesting that early sessions should avoid provoking increased levels of anxiety in husbands. Structured interventions may be more helpful in preventing premature therapy termination.

Remarried couples are also likely to have somewhat different treatment concerns. They may be less willing to tolerate a poor relationship, or their relationships with ex-spouses and stepchildren may need to receive a significant amount of attention early in therapy.

Differences in *values and belief systems* are also important. Good topics for study may be sex role and religious orientation, among others. Sex roles are very likely to affect the course of marital therapy since many basic elements of couples' interactions are grounded in their beliefs about good and proper husband and wife marital role behavior.

The same can be said for similarity and differences in religious orientation. Given that having a similar religious orientation was found to be important in at least one study of divorce prediction (Newfield, 1985), the issue of shared values and beliefs may be important in developing differential treatment approaches for the variety of couples who seek treatment.

Just as psychotherapy research in general has attempted to identify client variables related to treatment outcome (Garfield, 1994), the same must be true for marital therapy research in the future. Only by understanding the needs of different couples can marital therapists increase their effectiveness.

6

BASIC CONSIDERATIONS

FOCUS ON INTERACTION, NOT INTRAPERSONAL PROCESSES

Marital therapy is different from individual therapy in several ways. The main difference lies in the focus and emphasis on the pattern of the interaction between the partners, as opposed to the intrapsychic processes of the individuals. The unit of interest is what happens between the spouses or what happens in the sequence of behavior, rather than why persons are the way they are, or why they do what they do.

An individually oriented therapist might say, "Couples can have a good relationship only when both are healthy themselves." An interactionally oriented therapist would say, "The focus of treatment is on what the partners do in relation to each other." Again, the emphasis is on the interacting unit, not the intrapersonal processes of the individual spouses.

This is not to say that there is *no* interest in what happens within each individual; many times these issues become critically important. Rather, the emphasis on interaction is just that, an emphasis. The goal is to look primarily to the interaction of the couple system, then secondarily to the individuals within the relationship system.

Marital therapy is also different from individually oriented therapy with both spouses present because the emphasis is still on the couple's interaction, not the personal issues of each partner.

ASSUMPTIONS ABOUT BEHAVIOR

An interactional perspective also makes certain assumptions about behavior. First, it is assumed that most behavior is nonpathological. The concern is not about the diagnosis of personality traits or even most psychopathology; rather, it is on the effects of the interaction between the partners.

Second, an interactional perspective also emphasizes the idea that thoughts, feelings, and actions are primarily environmentally rather than intrapsychically driven. Therefore, the responsibility for change in the relationship belongs to each partner. They are responsible for their own actions and the consequences of these actions.

Third, couples often underestimate their own power to influence one another. Often, a feeling of helplessness can develop over time as spouses' attempts to affect their partner's actions are not productive; hence, frustration may develop. Unproductive attempts repeated over time will often lead partners to believe they are unimportant or powerless in their marriage. In actuality, however, spouses have a great deal of influence over the feelings of the other and can act as powerful agents to reward or punish each other. The power of each partner to impact the other may be demonstrated by an analysis of the sequences of behavior in a series of problematic interactions. Many times partners are unaware of the impact of their own behavior on their partner; rather they tend to see only the effects of their partners' behavior on themselves.

Fourth, focusing on interaction patterns implies less blame than does focusing on individual pathology and intrapsychic processes. However, it does not deemphasize the importance of individual responsibility for decisions, actions, and their consequences. Couples may be locked into a strong interaction pattern, but they can, ultimately, break the pattern and behave in more effective ways.

Fifth, the emphasis on patterns represents a conceptual shift from an individual perspective to a relationship and interactional focus. Therefore, it can be a difficult transition for those trained in individually oriented psychotherapeutic perspectives. Instead of identifying the diagnosis of each person, the question now must become "How are person A and person B mutually influencing each other?"

Assessment, then, is not focused on the pathology or personality variables of the individuals in the marriage. Rather, it focuses on the reciprocal patterns of interaction that couples have developed. Often this pattern can be most readily identified around such issues as power, disagreements, trust, intimacy, sex, and sex roles.

BEGINNING AN INTERACTIONALLY BASED ASSESSMENT OF POWER, TRUST, AND INTIMACY

How Spouses Deal with Power

1. To assess how clients deal with power, ask questions without directing them at one specific partner to see who answers for whom. Many times, the issue of power can be identified in the couple's discussion with the therapist. The dominant spouse may be the one who does most of the talking.

2. Another possibility is to observe who interrupts whom. The most powerful partner may be the one who can successfully interrupt and correct the other spouse's statements during the interview session.

3. Who decides about money? This issue can be constructively observed in the session when the charge for

the session is discussed and the fee paid. Spouses vary in their ideas about payment. Some may want the "unhappy spouse" to pay from personal funds. This implies an unequal interest in therapy and a possible unequal balance of power in the relationship. On the other hand, the couple may pay from the "family account." This may imply a more equal commitment to therapy and possibly a more equal balance of power in the relationship. Still others may alternate payments from one source to another. This may imply an equal relationship, but it may also hint at a rigid structure that has developed as a way to handle disagreements between the partners.

4. Who schedules the appointments? The person who does the scheduling is often the most invested in the process. If the other partner is less interested in therapy, it may become apparent in who calls for the initial appointment, or who calls to change or reschedule appointments during the course of treatment.

Scheduling difficulties may also reveal issues of power. First, there are problems that arise around the more powerful person's schedule. The more powerful partner may not have time to attend therapy or may want less frequent visits. That partner may also insist on appointment times that are very inconvenient for the other partner or for the therapist. Second, problems in keeping appointments may develop as well. The most powerful spouse is often the one who has the most problems in scheduling or attending therapy sessions. Here the principle of "least interest" can be seen to operate. This idea, common to social psychology, asserts that the person with the least interest in the outcome of counseling may maintain a greater power than the member who has the most interest in resolving the problems in the relationship.

How Spouses Deal with Disagreement

Watch the interaction when the partners disagree about something in the session. Does one partner "give in" more readily than the other? If one spouse does so consistently, this tendency may help to identify the power structure of the relationship. The person most willing to "give in" may be the less powerful member of the dyad. This may or may not be a problem for the couple; it depends on whether or not the weaker partner is happy or unhappy with that role.

When the couple has conflict, how does it end? There are three likely patterns. First, there are couples who seem to be able to resolve their disagreements after a period of intense conflict. This conflict may be difficult at times, but if they are able to stick to the issue at hand, they can frequently reach a satisfactory understanding.

The second pattern tends to emphasize an almost endless discussion about problems. In these cases, the couple can discuss their problems for hours, but they almost never can reach a resolution to them. Here the problem is that the couple has no way to effectively resolve their disagreements; they are unable or unwilling to compromise, give and take, or fully understand their partner. Often, the pattern is based on argument and counterargument rather than argument, understanding, and counterargument.

The third common pattern shown by some couples is where one or both partners withdraw from the disagreement and refuse to engage in a continued discussion. In these cases, the withdrawing partner may be demonstrating a helpless or hopeless position and may simply refuse to continue what he or she considers to be a painful discussion. Such cases are usually sincere demonstrations of hopelessness. There are a few instances, however, when the nonengaging partner has developed this strategy as a way of gathering power. In such cases, an unwillingness to participate in discussions may be a simple way for one partner to avoid facing responsibility for problems or giving in on any level to the other.

Understanding the difference between those who feel hopeless and those who are power seeking can be difficult. One can arrive at the best judgment by observing the couple's interactions on the issues cited earlier in this chapter. A withdrawn spouse who is never willing to engage in meaningful discussion of any relevant issue may be attempting to gain power over the other partner (and often the therapist) by refusing to become involved in the process. On the other hand, a reluctant partner who can be encouraged to express ideas and concerns is probably not seeking such power.

Overall, the more the couple is able to come to some sort of resolution themselves, however inefficiently, the better the prognosis for the case. The difficult cases are spouses who are more likely to demonstrate an intense disinterest in seeking to understand each other. Instead, they are more interested in justifying themselves, in proving their partners to be wrong, and in establishing blame for the hurt and pain they experience.

Do Spouses Trust Each Other?

Questions that can be useful in assessing this issue include the following: Can the partners trust each other on a day-to-day basis? Do they keep their word to each other? Are they dependable? Can they trust each other with sensitive information or secrets?

Considering questions of this nature helps therapists to identify where couples fall on a continuum of trusting one another. Couples with a long history of disappointments, anger, and humiliation are often quite reluctant to trust each other. However, at least a willingness to trust and the ability to risk a degree of vulnerability are necessary for spouses to develop confidence in one another. This is not always an easy task, but learning where the partners stand on this issue is very helpful in determining a plan for treatment.

In almost all cases, partners who have developed a strong sense of mistrust will be more difficult to treat, since learning to trust one another is a fundamental issue in a stable relationship.

How Spouses Handle Intimacy

How spouses handle intimacy is closely associated with their ability to trust. Observations about what level of emotional involvement is evident in the couple are informative about their relationship strengths. Key areas to explore in this domain are the expression of emotions, personal information, and day-to-day experiences that are important to them. The more intimate partners are with one another (assuming they desire the same level of intimacy), the more satisfied they are likely to be in their relationship.

Do They Agree About Sex?

Sexual expression is also closely related to trust and intimacy. In general, the more that trust and intimacy are important to the couple, the more the impact is evidenced in their sexual relationship. For most couples, the greater the trust and intimacy, the greater the degree of agreement about sexual issues.

Questions that can help one learn about the couple's adjustment in this area include: Do they agree about their sexual preferences and activities? Can they be affectionate outside of sex? Is there pressure to perform?

Do They Agree About Gender Roles?

Disagreements about gender-role expectations lend themselves to a whole range of misunderstandings and miscommunications. For example, for highly traditional men providing economically for their families is a fundamental value. This value, however, may conflict with their partner's expectations about spending time together, or being involved in such family activities as child care, schoolwork, and housework. It is often necessary to assess and address the issues of differences in perceptions about what constitutes good and desirable behavior for men and women.

Questions that may be helpful in gathering information regarding spouses' beliefs about gender roles include: Do they agree about good and proper behavior in their role as husband or wife? What are a man's duties and responsibilities and what are a woman's? In general, those who agree seem to do better than those who disagree.

7

COMMON ERRORS IN EFFECTIVE MARITAL THERAPY

For a therapist who is beginning to work with couples, several common mistakes need to be identified and avoided. This chapter will identify six of the most common mistakes and explain why these activities are mistakes and how they can have a negative impact on therapy. Finally, suggestions will be presented for avoiding these mistakes.

MISTAKE NO. 1: TAKING SIDES

One of the most common mistakes that therapists make in working with couples is deliberately or inadvertently establishing a coalition with one member of the couple. These coalitions can lead to the disengagement of the outside member of the couple, thus destroying a therapeutic alliance with both spouses.

Cases of Deliberate Side Taking

The therapist's deciding a priori who is to blame for the couple's difficulties is an example of deliberate side taking. This judgment may occur after hearing about the presenting problem from one spouse (such as in an intake process) or possibly from having a personal bias against women, men, or certain types of people in general. For example, hearing one partner refer to the other as abusive or cruel, or indifferent can lead many beginning therapists to form early and ill-advised conclusions.

The disease model or individual deficit perspective can also lead to side taking. For example, seeking to identify a diagnostic problem in one spouse or the other may lead the therapist to assume an excessive degree of knowledge about the person's attitudes, beliefs, and willingness to change. In labeling a person as "histrionic," a therapist might develop a negative attitude toward that partner.

Cases of Inadvertent Side Taking

A possible scenario is one in which the spouse wants to spend time on the telephone with the therapist discussing the problem, blaming the other spouse, or giving background. Such an interaction might provide some persuasive information or present the perspective of the partner on the phone in a convincing manner without input from the other partner, which could lead to inadvertent side taking.

In another scenario one spouse asks to be seen individually first. This is advisable in some cases, but it is often inappropriate since it might induce a coalition and alienate the nonparticipating spouse. In most cases, couples can be persuaded to attend therapy together once the idea has been explained to them.

How to Encourage Couples to Attend Together

1. Ask the participating spouse, "Have you asked him/her to come with you?"
2. If the answer is no, ask, "Would you be willing to ask?"

3. If the partner is reported to be unwilling, explain the difficulty it may cause in the future if you then are able to bring them in together.

4. The therapist can personally invite the reluctant spouse to participate. This contact may provide an opportunity to address the person's concerns and may be a useful intervention by itself.

What to Do When a Person Insists on Temporarily Being Seen Alone

Sometimes, despite all of the efforts of the couple's therapist, it becomes necessary to see one member first or run the risk of losing the case altogether. If this occurs, it is appropriate to see them individually, but when the time comes to introduce the absent spouse into treatment, the therapist must clearly address the issue of side taking to avoid the appearance of being more sympathetic toward the original client. This is best done in a direct manner by explaining that this is a common problem in seeing a second spouse later in treatment. For example, a therapist might say: "I am likely to be perceived as being on the side of your partner. It is not my intention to be so; rather, my priority is the interaction between people, not the assessment of the assignment of blame to one or the other. If you see a problem developing or get such an impression, would you let me know?" Asking the previously absent spouse to report or comment on any perception of unfair or uneven treatment or attention to either member will often nullify these concerns.

This approach is not recommended because the therapist then becomes the confidant of each spouse and may become privy to some confidential information from one or both of the spouses. In these cases, confidentiality becomes difficult as the therapist often struggles to remember which information must be confidential and which is not. For example, most professionals would consider revealing information about the background or behavior of the client partner to the other nonclient partner to be unethical. The same concerns exist when a therapist is treating a married couple. Would there not be the possibility of information from one partner being revealed to the therapist when it would be best done in the context of the couple? Common examples include one spouse's plans for divorce or separation, one spouse's relationship with a third party, the possibility of crimes or indiscretions having been committed (or being planned) by one party, gambling, and chemical dependencies.

To avoid being involved in such ethical dilemmas, when and if it becomes necessary to see spouses separately, it is best to insist that there be an explicit agreement of nonsecretiveness between the parties. In other words, all of what the therapist hears has to be considered fair game for discussion in future conjoint meetings. This strategy is usually acceptable to couples and allows the therapist to avoid an ethical straight jacket.

There are some situations in which a couple may not agree to this arrangement. One partner may feel that there is something that he or she wishes to discuss in a strictly private manner. In such cases, the limits of confidentiality need to be very clear with both partners; a goal of therapy will be to help the spouse with the confidential information to share it in a couple therapy setting.

What to Do When One Person Must Be Seen Alone for Marital Concerns

There are times when the second member of the couple is simply not willing to attend therapy, regardless of the spouse's or the therapist's intentions. In these cases, the focus of treatment can still be on the interaction of the two people. This can be accomplished by asking questions designed to identify the interaction patterns between the partners. Asking questions such as "What happened next?" or "What was after that?" can lead the spouse who is present to a better understanding of the patterns between the two spouses and possibly to his or her role in developing and maintaining the problem(s).

In addition, the focus of treatment can be on the behavior of the client in relation to the other spouse. For example, through an examination of the consequences of the client's actions, the partner's reactions can be studied. The client is not able to control the behavior of the partner, but certainly controls his or her own behavior, and by so doing directly influences the partner's behavior in return. The idea of reciprocity is evident here. Reciprocity refers to the tendency of spouses to respond to their partners in a manner consistent with the behavior their partners have directed toward them (Griffin & Crane, 1986). The goal of therapy in this case could be for the therapist to first help the client with a change in behavior, and then, relying on the tendency of the other partner to reciprocate, to cause a change in the behavior of the nonclient spouse. For example, one spouse could examine his or her own contribution to a coercive interaction pattern and decide to not continue to fuel the fire. This decision could interrupt the negative interaction pattern and allow other more positive behavior to emerge.

A third scenario that can lead to inadvertent side taking involves therapists' personal issues predisposing them to a particular orientation toward the couple. For example, therapists who have a history of difficult or abusive relationships may somehow see members of their own gender as victims. Conversely, therapists who consider their own relationships to be of high quality may prescribe their own values and choices to be a necessary part of most, if not all, other relationships. Hence, therapists may be predisposed to appear to agree with certain spouses and not others.

Therapists' discomfort with conflict or the intense emotions often expressed in working with couples may lead them to separate the couple by scheduling separate meetings with each. Such an approach will certainly control the level of conflict therapists experience in their office, but does little to help the couple to resolve their own problems.

Ways to Avoid Establishing Early Coalitions

1. Limit early telephone contacts to brief descriptions and arrangements. This makes the opportunities for coalition building less available to either party. If callers want to explain their situation in great detail, a simple request that they save this information for the first meeting is often sufficient to postpone long conversations.

2. Ask to see both spouses together at each meeting. By so doing, the therapist directly communicates the desirability of this action. As a result of the assumption that both will be present, many spouses who have been reluctant to address their concerns with their partner begin to do so.

3. Ask both partners to describe their own perspective; don't let one partner dominate the conversation. It will sometimes be necessary to respectfully stop one partner from talking while encouraging the other to speak. Suggestions such as "Why don't we see what Don thinks about this?" or "We'll get right back to that issue; let's see what Sue sees as important." might be helpful.

4. Ask a fairly equal number of questions of each partner and ask both partners to comment on each question in turn. This shows both partners that each of their perspectives is valued and will be included.

5. Match the frequency and duration of eye contact with both partners. Eye contact usually denotes attention and interest to each partner, so watching one person more intently than another may give the wrong impression.

6. Avoid seating arrangements that place the therapist in closer proximity to one spouse than to an-

other. Studies on physical proximity show that people who like each other are more likely to sit together (e.g., Crane et al., 1987). Consequently, unequal distance may denote an unequal relationship with the partners.

MISTAKE NO. 2: ALLOWING EMOTIONAL DUMPING

Oftentimes, couples who are distressed will have developed very low levels of discussion and interaction. Others will have developed a pattern of husband withdrawal and wife confrontation or vice versa. In each of these situations, it is necessary to structure the early therapy experience to prevent the tendency to complain, confront, or list problems and grievances for each spouse. Husbands who are withdrawn emotionally are especially sensitive to this problem: in many cases they will see therapy as threatening, a place where they will be confronted about their own inadequacies. It is almost always wives who seek therapy, and it is often husbands' discomfort that leads to early dropping out of therapy (Allgood & Crane, 1991). Although one common task in the early stages of therapy is to establish the presenting problem(s), it is important not to allow therapy to become a time of unrestrained complaining, griping, and criticizing of either spouse. This does not mean that conflict or emotional expression is not allowed, but rather that the emphasis is on preventing a one-sided discussion of complaints and criticisms directed at one partner.

One way to prevent emotional dumping from occurring is to establish the ground rules of therapy early. Clearly identifying what is expected will set the stage for the therapist's maintaining an active role in directing the process of therapy.

MISTAKE NO. 3: BECOMING A SEER

Some couples who request therapy are seeking the very best advice from an expert to find the solution to their problems or to determine who is "at fault." It is usually more effective if the couple takes responsibility for addressing their own issues with each other in a constructive manner. The goal is for the couple to work out issues, not for the therapist to be the "expert" who dispenses decisions.

Why Giving Opinions and Advice Often Doesn't Help

1. People remember what they want to remember, and spouses often remember different things about their therapy sessions. Many highly distressed couples will selectively remember the advice that is given and use it against each other. For example, one spouse might say, "The therapist said we should spend more time together. Why won't you stay home?"

2. Sometimes people seeking therapy are really seeking someone who will agree with their opinion on some fundamental issues. Typically, the couple's differing opinions about issues are in direct opposition with one another. Often, the beliefs held by the partners are mutually exclusive. For example, a wife wants her husband to be more expressive toward her; at the same time the husband wants her to give him more private time. In other words, both things can't happen at the same time. Appearing to recommend one idea over the other can alienate either party.

3. Some spouses begin counseling but are looking for a way out of continuing therapy. These partners may be waiting for an excuse to be offended, and giving advice at the wrong time may provide them with that excuse.

4. Some people have a tendency to avoid taking responsibility for their own actions, and they may look to the therapist to make a decision for them. The consequence is that the therapist becomes responsible for the outcome of the decision, rather than the spouses.

How to Avoid Answering Direct Questions About Advice or Judgments Regarding Blame

The idea is not to avoid responsibility for how therapy is conducted or to put off honest inquiries. Rather, it is to redirect such inquiries back to the couple so that they can begin to discuss the issues together. The goal is for them to reach some sort of common understanding about the problem and then, working together, to develop some possible solutions to the problem.

Explain that the goal is for them to reach a compromise about the problems they face. Then, direct the couple to discuss the issue together in the here and now of the session.

Ask "What have you tried so far?" and "What has worked well, and what hasn't?" Spouses may be able to identify past solutions to their concerns that may be applied to the present situation.

Redirect the question to the couple. For example, "What do you think about that, Jim?" The goal here is to get the couple to discuss the problem with each other.

MISTAKE NO. 4: DEALING WITH SEXUAL ISSUES TOO EARLY IN THERAPY

There are often substantial differences in the ways that the partners think and feel about their sexuality. These differences are often clustered around issues of caring and emotional intimacy. The conditions for affection and intimacy must be created before direct discussion about sexual matters can be done successfully. These conditions include establishing a degree of confidence, and the ability of the couple to trust one another. Once the emotional tone of the relationship has achieved the level of intimacy necessary, sexual issues can be dealt with in a safe environment. The emotional tone of the session and the feedback from both spouses can guide the therapist in deciding when to approach the couple about such issues.

MISTAKE NO. 5: THERAPIST UNAWARENESS OF GENDER ISSUES IN COUPLE THERAPY

Obviously, therapists bring to therapy their own gender. The awareness of one's assumptions and beliefs about gender should be carefully considered. For example, what are appropriate roles for men and for women in relationships? Different therapists would answer this question very differently; and the answers would be based on their own beliefs and values. Also, the objectives in therapy may differ considerably depending on the therapist's own personal values and beliefs. For example, some therapists may consider traditional role-oriented marriages to be inherently weak or oppressive to women and may think these sorts of marriages need to be changed to other more egalitarian forms. Yet this perspective ignores the fundamental question of whether or not this structure meets the needs of the specific couples in treatment. There is a wide range of types of marriages in which couples consider themselves to be happy. As some of those relationships are very traditional, should couples who have traditional marriages necessarily be encouraged to change their view? The reverse, of course, also occurs when couples in androgynous relationships seek therapy and encounter a therapist who holds more traditional views.

Again, the idea is not that therapy can be value-free. Rather, the issue is that therapists need to be aware of their own values, assumptions, and beliefs so that the interaction of their values and beliefs with those of the couples they treat can be carefully considered. In any event, the therapist should respect couples' preferences in this regard.

Therapists' views about relationships are often revealed in sessions by the following:

1. Who is spoken to in the interview first? In general, a consistent pattern of asking one person may reveal an attitude of preference or deference.

2. Who is allowed to interrupt whom? It is not unusual to inadvertently allow a more powerful spouse to interrupt the other. Being careful to balance talk time and question asking will prevent this from happening.

3. Who is allowed to answer for whom? Those who are more powerful may be quite willing to answer for their partner. Watch for those who resent their partner for doing this.

4. Who speaks first? Again, the issue is deference and preference. Be sure to balance the views of each party.

5. With whom does the therapist seem to agree the most often? Regardless of the best of intentions by the therapist, spouses will often make assumptions about the side they think the therapist is on. It is not uncommon for intense discussion and debate to occur between sessions as both spouses seek to invoke the agreement of the therapist on their side of the issue.

Other important issues related to gender are the different responses to therapy and different interaction processes that are evident for men and women. For example, men are more likely than women to (1) withdraw in the face of intense negative affect (Gottman, 1994a) and (2) attempt to limit conflict by appealing to rationality and compromise (see Raush, Barry, Hertel, & Swain, 1974). Women, on the other hand, are more likely to attempt to engage their partner in continued discussions (e.g., Gottman & Levenson, 1988). Thus it is important to be gender sensitive, anticipating different reactions to therapy by each partner and respecting the differences.

MISTAKE NO. 6: TRYING TO DO INDIVIDUAL THERAPY WITH BOTH SPOUSES PRESENT

This mistake occurs when the therapist tries to conduct individual interviews even when both partners are present in the therapy room. This is a mistake because the emphasis of therapy becomes the interaction of the therapist with each spouse instead of the interaction between the partners. This error by the therapist can occur in several ways:

1. The therapist may concentrate on what the spouses individually say they need or want as compared to what both need and what can be negotiated between them. In other words, "How can person A have his or her needs met?" instead of "How can each of you win, or get what you would like?"

2. Sometimes therapists err by talking primarily to each spouse in turn instead of stimulating the couple's discussion of important issues. This can be thought of as coaching or teaching partners how to solve their own problems through direct interaction as opposed to interviewing each spouse separately but with the partner in the room. Ideally, the therapist should encourage the couple to discuss issues together.

3. The therapist may seek a diagnosis for each person, instead of focusing on the interaction patterns between the spouses that may be leading to the present difficulties. The use of individual psychopathology diagnosis with couples can lend itself to gender-related stereotyping by assigning one partner, many times the woman, a diagnosis.

In addition, the assignment of a diagnosis can stigmatize one spouse while ignoring other possible systemic explanations for the presenting problems. For example, one frequent perception held by men is that their wives are "crazy or unbalanced" when, in fact, the behavior they are describing as "crazy" is simply a difference in what men and women often consider to be appropriate emotional expression (e.g., "Little or none," for men and "Say what is on your mind, discuss it," for women).

Finally, the issue of diagnosis, although important in other contexts and in other situations, doesn't usually address the main focus of marital therapy, which is the interaction between spouses. Topics such as how they talk to each other, reach decisions, negotiate, and give and take in relation to one another are often more fruitful foci of treatment.

4. The therapist may focus on the individual issues each spouse brings to therapy at the wrong time. Such a focus may be appropriate, but only *after* the relationship issues between the spouses have been addressed. This allows the therapist to set the stage for therapy by defining the nature of the current problems as primarily relational in nature rather than intrapersonal.

Some might say that is it essential for each individual to be well adjusted before there can be a well-adjusted marriage; however, there is no real evidence that individual therapy prior to marital therapy is necessary or appropriate for couples. This is not to say that one should ignore the individual problems of the clients—this would be unrealistic. Rather, the focus of marital therapy should be on the relationship; the individual concerns, strengths, and issues of the couple are best considered in terms of how they impact the relationship. Then and only then can one delve into the treatment of more individually oriented concerns. For example, when a wife asks for help with depression, the first questions should be about the convergence of the depression and marital concerns. There is often considerable overlap, and the effect of her partner's behavior and attitudes should be addressed prior to (or along with) a more individually oriented approach to treating the depression. Many times, a marital therapy treatment can be very helpful in alleviating depressive symptoms in women (O'Leary & Beach, 1990).

8

THE PROCESS OF COUPLE THERAPY

The process of therapy can best be described as a series of simultaneous activities that merge and reflect the needs of both the couple and their counselor.

PRINCIPLE NO. 1: LEARN WHAT EACH PERSON WANTS

The first task of the therapy is to learn from both partners why they are seeking counseling. Often there are different answers to this question, reflecting different agendas for being in therapy and the different needs of each partner. The needs of both partners should be addressed almost simultaneously since the participation of both is required for successful treatment. Couples present with the following common agendas.

"What we really want is to stop fighting and to avoid a divorce."

These couples, with what is probably the most common of presenting problems, reflect a genuine concern for their relationship and simply want to stop hurting one another. They are often very willing to take risks and try new things and are still committed to their relationship. Couples with this agenda can most often be identified by their sincere efforts to hear what is being said and to learn new things, as well as by demonstrating these goals by behavior as well as by words. These couples have a very good prognosis for improving their relationship.

"We can't agree."

These couples can easily be identified because both partners are usually verbal and articulate about their concerns. In cases where both partners can articulate dissatisfactions or problems with their relationship, the task of the therapist is to carefully attend to and reflect the concerns of both parties. The therapist facilitates the couple's efforts to negotiate changes and compromises that reflect the needs of both partners. This task can become complicated when the perceived solutions for the problems of each partner seem mutually exclusive. In such cases compromise positions are hard to develop since the gain by one partner can be seen as a direct cost to the other.

"What we really want is to have more passion and romance in our marriage; we seem to have lost what we once had."

These couples can be identified by an absence of overt conflict and the presence of a great deal of loneliness and isolation. Their relationship can be described as a gradual decline, from high levels of interest, excitement, and interaction to the current low levels of the same. Even if their initial attraction to and interest in one another seem to have been replaced by life stress and nonrelationship priorities, these couples can learn to recapture some of what they had initially if they are willing to make time together and shared positive activities a priority in their lives. On the other hand, if they are unwilling to make the necessary time and sacrifices that this entails, they are placing serious limitations on their ability to make their relationship more interesting and energetic.

"He/she needs to change."

One of the most common patterns occurs when one partner seeks therapy to "change the other." In this case, the spouses are seeking an ally to influence their partner in a direction that they have already deemed necessary. These couples can most often be identified by the presence of one partner who has a long history of trying to change the other and a long list of things that need to be done by that partner.

This alliance seeking can be quite compelling if the co-alition-seeking partners are allowed to present their case for too long of a time. The danger of participating in this agenda too long is that the second partner, the "target to be changed," is likely to be offended or put off by the alliance of therapist and spouse, and may quickly become unwilling to participate in further sessions. Conversely, not taking the "change seeker" seriously enough can also lead to an early termination of treatment since this person is both the initiator and the motivator for seeking and continuing therapy.

On the other hand, many times the partner who would be changed is quite willing for things to continue as they are, and wishes to minimize the problems and change as little as possible. In this case, the partners can negotiate the best possible course between both sets of expectations, but it needs to be done carefully. The therapist should reflect a genuine interest in and recognition of each position, delicately balancing both sets of needs.

"What I really want is for you to take care of him/her after I leave."

This pattern can most often be identified by one partner's seemingly insincere participation in counseling. This is often manifest in an unwillingness to discuss concerns or changes he or she would like to see made in the relationship. Another clue is one partner's unwillingness to engage in meaningful homework assignments. Instead, that partner responds to such tasks by brushing them off, forgetting, or being too busy to work on them. Another possible sign is infrequent attendance at scheduled therapy sessions. In this case, one spouse will appear for the meeting, but the other partner supposedly will be unavoidably detained or will have a last minute so-called emergency that arises. A single instance of such behavior is not necessarily indicative of this agenda, but if repeated, it should be considered as a possibility.

Often, the goal of the insincere spouse is for the therapist and "spouse to be left" to establish a relationship that will endure after departure of the "leaver." The idea is to provide a person who will support the abandoned partner when the person leaving the relationship is no longer willing to do so. If the therapist suspects that this agenda may be in operation, a direct and candid discussion about the possibility is warranted.

"What I (we) really want is to for therapy to fail so that I (we) can tell others we tried everything."

Sometimes, one or both partners will already have made a decision to end their relationship prior to entering treatment. The exercise of therapy is then related to appeasing some other influential person or institution regarding the hopelessness of their situation. Such couples can be identified by an almost complete air of pessimism about the future of their relationship. Occasionally, they will make references to others who were influential in their seeking counseling and who seem to be important in determining the success or failure of their marriage. Examples include parents or other relatives, church or synagogue leaders, and others who are powerful influences in the lives of the couple. These persons can be instrumental in motivating some couples to seek counseling, and some couples will want to demonstrate their failure in therapy in order to justify or explain their divorce or separation. Again, if the therapist suspects that the couple is motivated primarily to pacify someone else, a straightforward discussion is in order.

"What we really want is to break up, and we would like some help with this difficult transition."

Couples in this category can be identified by how they explain their goals. If they are given an opportunity to be honest with each other and with the therapist, they will usually clearly identify their goals.

Such couples will then need help in working out what went wrong, in dealing with the hurt and anger associated with the breakup, and in working out difficult post-breakup issues such as custody, visitation, and child support. In these situations, the therapist can provide a valuable service by helping the couple through this difficult and painful set of transitions. For many couples, breaking up may be their best solution.

PRINCIPLE NO. 2: ESTABLISH CONTROL OF THE COUNSELING SESSION

The second general principle in the process of therapy is the requirement that the therapist needs to establish control of the process and content of the counseling sessions. The assumption is that if the couple had been able to discuss their concerns in a constructive and beneficial way, they would have done so prior to, or instead of, seeking counseling. People can argue or dump on each other at home. One goal of therapy is for the couple to have a better experience in counseling than they would have had on their own. (Why else should they pay for the service?) If left on their own, most couples have the tendency to do things that are not very helpful in resolving their concerns. Consequently, it is important for the therapist to maintain control of the session.

Deciding When to Control Escalating Emotions

Not all emotional expression is harmful, nor is it all necessarily helpful. The therapist must decide on an appropriate balance of maintaining control of highly charged affect, and remaining patient when the partners are struggling to say what is on their minds. The idea is not that arguing, persuading, disagreement, and the like are to be minimized, but rather that conflict needs to be managed in an attempt to focus on resolution. Indeed, some evidence suggests that "conflict engagement" is helpful in maintaining long-term relationship satisfaction (Gottman & Krokoff, 1989).

The best rule of thumb is that if it looks as though someone is going to get hurt, stop it. The goal is to prevent exchanges that are unnecessarily hurtful or destructive. Watch the reactions of both partners to see what their threshold for anger and emotional turmoil might be. Couples will usually show their discomfort level by their nonverbal behavior, including facial expressions such as grimacing, deflecting intensity by avoiding eye contact, or withdrawing from the interaction. Other symptoms of stress include changes in physiological arousal such as increased heart and breathing rate and perspiration. All of these features are associated with an unpleasant and aversive body state called diffuse physiological arousal (Gottman, 1994a). Diffuse physiological arousal is important in therapy because couples who demonstrate higher levels of arousal during conflict situations are more likely to escalate conflict, to retaliate with negative actions, and to have lower levels of marital satisfaction and stability over the long run (e.g., Levenson & Gottman, 1985). Consequently, as couples slip into higher levels of conflict over extended periods, their chances of improved marital interaction patterns and satisfaction with therapy are likely to decrease.

How to Prevent Escalations and When It Is Important to Do So

Since the escalation of negative interaction is a common characteristic of distressed couples, it is necessary in many situations to prevent these escalations from occurring in the therapy sessions. This can be done in several ways. First, explain at the beginning of therapy the expectations of emotional control and, if necessary, that the therapist may interrupt escalations during sessions.

Second, be sure to balance the amount of time each spouse talks in the session so that one partner doesn't monopolize the time available by complaining and criticizing the other partner. When this process is allowed to occur without interruption, it is often likely that one partner will feel punished and singled out for blame. Blamed partners may retaliate by increasing their own negative interaction; such retaliation is likely to produce a reciprocal negative interaction from the other partner. These negative interactions then increase the probability of future negative interactions, such as complaining and blaming, name calling, and rehashing the past. If left unchecked, these behavior patterns will lead to more emotional escalations and negative conflicts in future sessions.

Therapists also need to limit the degree to which spouses are allowed to complain about and criticize their partner. This does not mean that spouses can't discuss their concerns or voice their complaints; rather, it is a matter of degree and emphasis. Instead of allowing one partner to dominate the discussion with complaints, both partners should be allowed approximately equal time to express themselves and to respond to their partner's concerns. Additionally, instead of spouses spending all of their time complaining about the other, there should also be some time for positive exchanges and statements of appreciation.

How to Diffuse Eruptions When They Occur

There are a number of techniques a therapist can use to control sessions, to intervene, to manage conflict when it is excessive, and to direct the session in ways that are more therapeutic.

The easiest, and probably the simplest, way to control a session is simply to point out the goals and expectations of the session. By making positive statements and by imposing a structure on the meeting, therapists send the message that they are in charge of the events that will occur.

A second method of controlling the session is to use humor, for example, identifying a negative interaction that is occurring by pointing it out and making it mildly humorous. For instance, "Is this something that happens at home? How helpful is it? Would you like to continue or would you like to go on in another direction?" In most cases, this mild sort of confrontation, when presented in a humorous and lighthearted way, will diffuse the emotional exchange. Therapists can redirect the session in the way they would like it to go.

Another, and more assertive, way of controlling the session is to point out when negative interactions are occurring and to ask the couple if they would like to continue the session or not. If they resist the attempt to diffuse the situation, then the therapist can resort to more severe methods. For example, "If you wish to continue to fight in this session, I can just leave" or "Would you like to leave now instead of continuing this session? I have no interest in observing and watching you hurt each other, and if you are going to continue, please do so on your own time."

PRINCIPLE NO. 3: INDUCE INTERACTION BY HAVING THEM TALK TO EACH OTHER, NOT TO THE THERAPIST

In general, try to induce interaction between the partners by having them talk to each other rather than to the therapist. This can be done by asking the couple to speak to each other about their concerns. The therapist can then observe and influence the interaction in ways that are more productive. For example, couples who are being taught how to listen better can be shown how to maintain eye contact and how to validate the speaker's feelings and point of view. The speaker, on the other hand, can be taught how to present concerns in nonthreatening and nonjudgmental ways, such as by first introducing a positive topic for discussion, or by reframing the concern into a neutral statement. For example, instead of one spouse's saying "You're irresponsible with money," the therapist can help the speaker say the same thing in a less threatening way, such as "I know that you're as concerned about money as I am" or "I know we disagree about how to handle our money. Can we talk about a compromise?"

Having the couple address each other in discussing problems early in the session will usually lead to a feeling that they've learned to understand each other better and have a new, although somewhat fledgling, ability to discuss problems more effectively. An exception to the rule of inducing interaction occurs when couples are highly volatile or negative, and when escalations are likely to take place. In those situations, it is sometimes necessary to have the spouses speak directly to the therapist and have the therapist reflect the intent and meaning of what is being said to the other spouse. This defuses the interaction and slows it down so that the highly reactive and negative interaction cycles typical of highly distressed couples do not automatically occur in the session.

PRINCIPLE NO. 4: LOOK FOR BALANCE OF POWER, INTIMACY, AND TRUST

Observation of basic issues of marital interaction (as mentioned in Chapter 4) can sometimes best be done by focusing on the three basic issues of power, intimacy, and trust. Basic issues of power and control sometimes manifest themselves in presenting problems relating to communication, sexual expression, or financial management. Since power and control are often exhibited in daily interaction in these three areas, problems with one or more of these subjects might involve issues of power and control.

Intimacy issues in relationships are often presented as loneliness and distance between one another or a fear of intimacy, or mistrust. Fear of intimacy can occur either from a history of difficult past relationships or as a consequence of the current relationship. In cases of fear of intimacy being related to past relationships, the therapist needs to spend time discussing the influence of the early relationships, whether in the family of origin or in difficult adolescent or adult interactions. It may be necessary to resolve these issues before proceeding to help the couple to establish more intimacy in their current relationship. The ability to trust one another seems to be directly related to the accumulation of positive and negative experiences between spouses. For example, misrepresentation of previous history or facts; unreliability in employment; inconsistent attitudes and behavior toward children or toward other people; jealousy; extramarital relations; or dishonesty in business, personal, or financial matters can sometimes accumulate in a relationship and lead to a lack of trust between partners. A lack of trust, then, can subsequently lead to negative interactions and conflict because of the necessity of checking and double-checking the stories that are told by one partner to another.

PRINCIPLE NO. 5: LOOKING FOR ATTRIBUTION

It is very helpful to try to understand what both partners believe to be the causes of the problems they are experiencing. If they attribute the problem solely to the behavior and attitudes of the other partner, the treatment becomes very difficult. If they're willing to accept responsibility for part of the problem themselves, and they attribute the cause of their problems to something other than their partners' bad nature or evil intent, the process of therapy is usually much easier.

The purpose of assessing attribution is to identify any global and stable negative attributions about the partners and their relationship that might exist. Global and stable negative attributions about the partners and the relationship seem to be important in the long-term development of marital stability or instability (see Gottman, 1994a) and generally interfere with the process of therapy if not addressed directly. The interference of these attributions takes the form of noncompliance with therapeutic tasks and a persistent, negative interpretation of the other partner's behavior or intentions. For example, a spouse's response toward the other partner's behavior may be determined not by the behavior itself, but by the spouse's general sentiment toward that partner. A persistent pattern of generally negative sentiment toward one partner will often result in highly reactive, negative interaction in which the spouses observe, in a hypervigilant manner, the behavior of their partner and then overreact to things that their partner does.

An example of this sort of problem occurs when events that transpire between spouses are described by both spouses in highly subjective, negative terms implying meanness and bad intent on the part of their partner. This creates a climate of negative interaction and anticipated criticism and punishment that can lead both partners to become increasingly sensitive to their partner's actions. There is also a greater tendency for both to criticize and punish the other based on the attributions or assumptions that they make about their partner's behavior, intentions, and personality.

For example, one study by Holtzworth-Munroe and Jacobson (1985) found that distressed couples engaged in more negative attributions than nondistressed couples. Whereas nondistressed couples engaged in relationship-enhancing attributions, distressed couples engaged in distress-maintaining attributions. These distress-maintaining attributions or cognitions were of two types: innocent victim or righteous indignation (Gottman, 1994a). Over time, these attributions become the filter through which spouses learn to perceive the behavior of their partner. Through filters of negative attribution events are interpreted as negative by distressed couples, while these same events will be interpreted as neutral (or even positive) by nondistressed partners.

Relationship-enhancing attributions, by contrast, tend to treat negative interactions as fleeting, situational, or temporary in nature. For example, a partner in a nondistressed couple may react to a negative interaction by thinking, "Oh well, she's in a bad mood," or "He must have had a hard day at work." Negative interactions in unhappy marriages, however, are often thought to be stable and internal to the partner, for example, "He is an inconsiderate and selfish person and that's the way he'll always be and there's nothing I can do to change it."

Relationship-enhancing attributions minimize the impact of negative behavior and enhance the impact of positive behaviors by the individual members of the partnership. In summary, distressed couples are more likely to attribute their partner's perceived negative behavior to permanent and unchangeable internal factors and personality traits such as stubbornness, laziness, or meanness. Nondistressed partners, on the other hand, are more likely to attribute their partner's negative behavior to factors such as "having a bad day."

PRINCIPLE NO. 6: LOOK FOR UNREALISTIC EXPECTATIONS OF SELF, EACH OTHER, AND THE RELATIONSHIP

Some couples come to marriage with unrealistic expectations about their partner and the process of marriage itself. Unrealistic expectations about marriage may include ideas about romantic love and emotional bonding. Some spouses expect to maintain a high degree of romantic love and high levels of intense intimacy, continuously and for a very long time. However, these expectations are not realistic over the course of a long-term relationship. Certainly, romance is present in relationships, but usually not at a level equal to that in the early stages of the relationship. One might ask if the spouses are expecting too much. Do they expect to make their partner happy in all things? At all times? Do they expect to have their partner meet all of their needs and never waiver? Do they expect to be deliriously happy with their relationship at all times?

Unrealistic expectations for partners often include such ideas as: "My partner should be able to tell when I want something"; "My partner should know what I really need"; "If my partner truly loves me, he (or she) should be able to make me happy"; and "My partner should have no other interests outside of me and our relationship."

Since relationships change over time, the level of emotion that is characteristic of the "honeymoon phase" is not likely to continue indefinitely. Instead, most couples find that their relationship becomes more interesting and satisfying than it was early on, but in different ways.

In work with couples with unrealistic expectations, the goal of therapy is to help the spouses to appreciate each other more fully. In addition, they may need to develop some similar interests and explore areas of shared interests. This may allow them to learn more about each other in new environments and spend more time in enjoyable, shared activities.

PRINCIPLE NO. 7: THE ROLE, PURPOSE, AND USE OF HOMEWORK ASSIGNMENTS

Homework assignments are tasks or activities assigned by the therapist for the couple to complete between sessions.

They should be used for a specific purpose and be clearly related to the couple's presenting problems. Homework should also be easily communicated and understandable to the couple. For example, if a couple is learning to express their feelings more directly to one another, a homework activity might be designed to have them practice such discussions between meetings. For another couple, the task might be related to increasing trust between the partners. In this case, the activity might be to have the partners list as many ways as possible that their spouse has honored a commitment made between them.

There can be a number of possible goals for homework assignments. A first therapeutic goal might be to help spouses to demonstrate their commitment to each other and their willingness to work on their relationship. In the first few sessions, a carefully designed commitment-based assignment can help to clarify the issue of commitment for both the therapist and the spouses. When completed, these assignments can provide a solid basis for optimism in working together. Assignments that are *not* completed should be handled as discussed in Chapter 10.

Second, assignments can also be given to translate what the couple experiences in therapy to their home environment. It is one thing to have a discussion or reach an understanding while in the safe confines of a therapist's office, but is quite another to have the same success while discussing problems at home. Many times this is a main therapy goal—to help the couple learn to have safe discussions and interaction at home.

Many couples can also benefit by having an opportunity to try new skills or ways of interacting through structured activities between sessions. As an example, it may be appropriate for some couples who have developed a great deal of isolation from one another to take time each evening for quiet sharing of the day's events and activities, to brush each other's hair, or to give each other a massage before bedtime.

Third, in sessions where there has been a positive exchange of information, or new insight given to one another, the therapist may ask that the discussion continue on the same topic between meetings. This may serve to help the couple increase their understanding of each other by continuing discussions after the session is over.

Some couples would like to feel a sense of control regarding their therapy experience. These couples often respond well to assignments between sessions because they often feel that they have something constructive to do between sessions. Home assignments in this case might involve the couple in developing lists of areas to discuss during each session, such as concerns they might have or things they like about each other.

There is also the possibility that having a couple work on skills or new experiences between sessions can speed up therapy. If all goes well between sessions, this may be a significant savings for them in terms of time and money.

How and When to Use Homework Assignments

One basic rule of thumb is to use assignments primarily *when you can anticipate what will happen* and when the outcome is likely to be positive. This is important because assignments can backfire, causing increased conflict and disappointments between couples. As a result, assignments need to be carefully planned to minimize the chance for a negative experience.

The planning of an assignment should take into consideration the requirements outlined in Chapter 10. The assignment should seem reasonable to the couple, should be clearly related to their ideas about their concerns, and should not require taking a step that is too large for them. The couple needs to be willing to commit to carrying out the assignment.

Couple vs. Individual Assignments

Individual assignments are tasks given to each partner separately. They are often used in cases where asking spouses to do things together is not yet possible because of mistrust, isolation, or high levels of conflict between the partners.

When individual assignments are given, it is important that they are balanced between spouses. For example, it is unwise to ask one spouse to do something for the other without making a reciprocal request to the partner. If this is not done, the targeted spouse may feel slighted, ignored, or unimportant in the process. Both spouses should have an assignment, and the assignments should be equal in terms of level of difficulty.

Never ask one spouse to do something difficult without asking the other partner for an equivalent level of effort. Otherwise the assignment may focus unfair attention on only one partner. Check carefully to see if the tasks seem fair to each person.

Also, never ask one spouse to do something that he or she is not freely willing to do. Be careful not to trust the client's initial response to a potential assignment. Many people have trouble setting boundaries with others (including the therapist) and may have difficulty objecting to an assignment even though it is uncomfortable or impossible. Always ask in several ways if an assignment makes sense, is understood, and, most importantly, is agreeable to both parties. Pressure or coercion directed toward one spouse will often result in assignment failures (at best) and dropping out early from therapy (at worst).

Couple assignments are given when there is a good prognosis for profitable interaction between the spouses. In these cases, the couple has shown some evidence of being able to interact effectively and has had some positive experiences in the therapy setting. Assignments are designed to be done together and usually can be accomplished only by some joint agreement. For example, an assignment for a husband to brush his wife's hair can be done only with her consent. Conversely, an assignment for the husband to spend more time with the children can usually be done with or without the wife's direct consent.

When Not to Give Assignments

Couples who are highly coercive, verbally or physically abusive, highly distressed, or for whom the exercise may create more conflict are poor candidates for homework assignments. Such couples can be identified by a high level of anger, sensitivity, or excessive vigilance associated with real or perceived provocations.

With these couples, assignments can be distorted by one partner as a means of establishing real or imagined injuries or insults. For example, many spouses in highly distressed relationships are extremely vigilant in observing and responding to their partner's behavior. Such highly vigilant partners may interpret any perceived failure to complete an assignment (in its entirety, to perfection) as a personal insult, and may respond accordingly. If the couple's pattern of interaction is characterized by such behavior, assignments will often do more harm than good, and should be avoided until the pattern of vigilant observation and reaction is changed.

Assignments should also not be given that are clearly beyond the couple's demonstrated abilities. Examples include asking couples who have no experience in positive sharing of feelings or ideas to do so on their own. Since they have not been able to share such feelings previously, they are likely to fail in this assignment.

A related mistake in giving assignments too quickly is to ask couples to have discussions about highly inflammatory or sensitive matters. In such cases, homework assignments should follow only successful interactions in the session. Spouses should never be assigned to do something they have not been able to do in the session. In fact, it may be appropriate in such cases for the couple to *cease* having discussions about their problems between sessions. The rationale is that if they were able to have such discussions in a beneficial manner, they probably would have done so prior to, or instead of, entering therapy. By continuing to discuss their problems in the same old ways, they are likely to simply repeat their ineffective or dysfunctional patterns. Assignments, then, need to be very simple and designed to decrease the conflict and tension they feel.

How to Evaluate the Usefulness of an Assignment After It Has Been Given

In general, homework assignments are used to help couples practice new skills and ways of interacting in their own day-to-day lives. The degree to which an assignment has been useful can be determined primarily by what is learned from the experience. Ask clients what happened, what they thought about the assignment, what they learned from doing it, what problems they encountered (if any), and so on to learn what effect it had. If it worked well, congratulate them on their efforts, and if it didn't, take the blame yourself first. (See Chapter 10 for further discussion about how to handle situations where assignments are not completed or where the couple is unable or unwilling to complete them.)

9

WHAT TO DO WITH MODERATELY DISTRESSED COUPLES

The purpose of this chapter is threefold: to discuss what is meant by "moderately distressed" couples; to examine the key ingredients for successful marital therapy (Alexander et al., 1994) noted in Chapter 3; and, finally, to present various ways in which these goals may be accomplished through the use of several possible intervention strategies.

IDENTIFYING MODERATELY DISTRESSED COUPLES

Moderately distressed couples can be identified by a relatively high level of commitment to each other and to the relationship and relatively low levels of destructive negative interaction cycles. Although negative affect is present, it is usually largely controlled and outbursts are rare. If a pretreatment assessment instrument such as the Marital Adjustment Test (MAT; Appendix A), the Dyadic Adjustment Scale (DAS; Appendix B), or the Revised Dyadic Adjustment Scale (RDAS; Busby, Crane, Larson & Christensen, 1995) is used, both members of these couples typically score in the range of 60 to 80 and above for the MAT, 32 to 45 and above on the RDAS, and 80 to 95 and above on the DAS (based on one standard deviation from the mean for couples presenting for marital therapy) (Crane et al., 1990). More severely distressed couples are identified as one standard deviation (or more) below the mean for clinical couples. Severely distressed couples (MAT of 60, RDAS of 32, or DAS of 80 or less) are generally less available for research purposes, and less is known about appropriate treatments for them (see Chapter 11).

On occasion marital partners will report very different levels of marital satisfaction. Large discrepancies (10 or more points on either scale) are difficult to interpret, as they can occur for two reasons. First, spouses usually view their relationship quite differently such that the satisfaction scores yielded on standard adjustment or satisfaction measures may vary. Second, some spouses use self-report assessment as a method of communicating the urgency of their concerns to their partner and to the therapist. The intent of the underreporting spouse is often to motivate or frighten the other partner into some action. In these cases, a spouse may report a very different level of satisfaction on these same assessments after only brief treatment. Consequently, these cases appear to be skewed in the direction of high distress, but they fall more accurately into the category of moderately distressed and respond quite well to treatment once the sense of urgency and pressure is relieved.

Moderately distressed couples are the type of couples who have usually been studied in the treatment outcome literature. As mentioned in Chapter 3, these couples can be treated by a number of different approaches. Most treatments, however, share several similar process and outcome goals that, although described differently according to the approach in question, are quite similar.

ESSENTIAL PROCESS AND OUTCOME GOALS FOR EFFECTIVE COUPLE THERAPY

Sharing Thoughts and Feelings

Sharing thoughts and feelings is important to all models. The principle is that couples need to slow down their process enough so that they can spend the time necessary to clearly understand each other. The sharing of thoughts and feelings can be accomplished by using interventions such as communication skills training and learning to talk about emotions.

Increased Emotional Engagement Between Spouses

In order to facilitate the goal of increased emotional engagement, the therapist must establish a safe and caring environment in each session. For couples to begin to feel a greater degree of emotional engagement, they must redevelop their ability to trust one another with thoughts and ideas that make them vulnerable. Couples can be brought to trust one another to the extent that (1) they express thoughts and feelings, (2) these thoughts and feelings are respected by their partner, and (3) there is some action toward problem resolution that occurs after these thoughts and feelings are expressed.

Increased Ability to Manage and Handle Negative Affect

All couples will experience conflict during their relationship. The presence of conflict is not an indication of relationship dysfunction; instead, the deciding factor may be how such conflict is handled. Functional relationships are able to manage conflict constructively; dysfunctional ones are not. As a result, almost all models of treatment try to include some provision for how couples will handle conflict and the negative affect associated with such contention.

It is often beneficial to help couples understand that conflict is inevitable in most close relationships, that such conflict is normal for most people, and that it is not a symptom of more serious problems per se. Also, conflict will not, by itself, inevitably overwhelm them. Even though their conflict can sometimes be quite painful, it can be resolved.

In addition, they need to have some successful experiences in managing negative affect when it occurs during the therapy sessions. Successful experience with the presence, management, and constructive resolution of conflict is essential for the couple to be able to handle such conflict in the future. In other words, they need to have positive experience in handling the inevitable disagreements and gripes that occur in everyday life.

Acceptance of Unresolvable Conflicts

Some differences that exist between people are going to be unchangeable. In this case, the goal would be to increase understanding about these issues, while allowing the couples to accept these things as they are. Good examples of such differences are basic values and core beliefs, and differences in temperament and personality.

How does one decide what issues are to be accepted and which are unacceptable? As discussed in Chapter 7, the best answer lies with each spouse and each couple.

Cognitive–Emotional Shifts

One main goal of therapy might be to produce less blaming and punishing behavior toward each spouse. This cognitive shift, from blaming to some degree of acceptance of differences, is so important that it should be considered as the essential first step in couple therapy. The process of changing attributions can be aided by therapist interventions such as making the implicit assumptions explicit, challenging unwarranted beliefs and suggesting alternative explanations.

Affective Changes (Changes Accompanied by Strong Affect)

Both insight oriented marital therapy and emotionally focused couple therapy have identified the experiencing of strong affect as an important ingredient in couple therapy. In addition, more recent behavioral marital therapy authors have also included an emphasis on emotion in treatment (e.g., Jacobson & Holtzworth-Munroe, 1986).

In some ways, this goal may be described as producing some sense of emotional relief in the therapy session. The emotional relief can be achieved by discussing deeply felt emotions, developing new insights regarding oneself and one's partner, understanding one another at a more intimate level, and expressing previously unexpressed fears and vulnerabilities (and having them respected). All of these activities can be vehicles for producing strongly felt affect and relief from previously unexpressed or painful emotions.

INTERVENTION TECHNIQUES TO ACCOMPLISH THE ESSENTIAL GOALS

Developing the Working Alliance or Collaborative Set

The essential first step is to develop a collaborative set or a working relationship with each spouse. This step seems to be important in every type of couple therapy, and should be considered the first priority, before moving on to other treatment procedures, regardless of what is done later.

The essential elements in developing this relationship include two key features. First, both members of the couple have to believe that the therapist listens, understands, and supports them. It is not possible to proceed successfully in couple therapy if this condition is not met. In demonstrating trustworthiness to both partners, it is essential to avoid the common mistakes mentioned in

Chapter 7. These will prevent the development of inadvertent alliances and side taking. Focusing on the relationship rather than on the weaknesses or fault of either partner can be very helpful.

The second essential element in developing a collaborative working alliance with the couple is for both spouses to learn to see their partner in a new light. This has a great deal to do with the attributions each partner makes of the other's behavior, motivations, intent, and personality. As long as these attributions are negative or critical of the spouse, little progress can be made in therapy. This is due to the very powerful effects such attributions have on the behavior of the partners (see Chapter 4). Spouses who believe that their partner is lying, lazy, dishonest, or the like will usually behave in a guarded manner toward their partner, which prevents positive interaction. In the best case, they are likely to be guarded, and in more difficult cases, they may be very critical and punishing towards their partner. Given that negative behavior is reciprocated at a high rate, and that the development of destructive negative interaction cycles is typical of most distressed couples, changing blaming attributions in order to interrupt these cycles is an important first step in therapy.

Gender Considerations in Selecting Intervention Strategies

The process of problem solving identifies a series of rules or procedures for problem resolution. As such it may particularly appeal to husbands, because it limits confrontation. Some authors have noted a gender-based pattern of couples' interaction where wives are more likely to bring up important relationship issues and husbands are more likely to withdraw from real or perceived conflict (Markman, 1991). In these situations, it may be important to consider the husband's anxiety (Allgood & Crane, 1991) by appealing to his need for structure and rules (e.g.,

Markman & Kraft, 1989). Thus the interventions of communication and problem-solving training may provide an important starting point for many couples.

Communication Training

Communication training is a hallmark of several approaches to therapy with couples. Each approach emphasizes somewhat different aspects of communication, but all contain some similar elements such as listening, paraphrasing, and nonverbal skills, including demonstrating attention, tracking, and showing agreement. In fact, some evidence seems to indicate that using the ingredients of active listening and expressive communication skills can be as effective as many of the other approaches to couple therapy (e.g., Ross, Baker, & Guerney, 1985).

The first step in communication training focuses on listening and speaking skills. *Listening* can be identified by several key spousal behaviors that the therapist can demonstrate and encourage even if communication training per se is not the focus of treatment. First, encourage maintaining eye contact while one's partner is speaking. This can best be done by a direct intervention such as, "Please look at each other as you discuss this issue." Second, help each partner to focus on what the other partner is saying instead of the more common reaction of planning a rebuttal. Again, direct instruction is helpful. For example, "We will have plenty of time to understand each side of the story. Right now though, I would like you to first show that you understand the other's position about these things by listening to one another very carefully." This does not mean that spouses will agree with what their partner is saying. Instead, their opportunity for presenting their side is guaranteed. The goal is to demonstrate and practice (in the context of current problems and concerns) that spouses can listen to and understand one another.

Listening is also important in overcoming the tendency of some husbands to resort to an emphasis on *rational discussion* when faced with their wife's distress. In these cases the husband's effort to solve the problem quickly may be misread by the wife as not caring about her feelings. As a result he may need to demonstrate his caring *simply by better listening* (rather than by rapidly proceeding to problem solving, or giving advice). Spending more time in listening demonstrates concern about the problem and feelings being expressed.

The role of speakers is to express themselves as clearly as possible, in a limited amount of time, and to avoid personal criticism and complaints. In order for this process to work, speaking partners need to express themselves in clear and short statements. Otherwise, their partner will become overloaded on the information being presented and will be unable to reflect the intent and meaning accurately. Consequently, ask the speakers to be fairly brief in the expression of their concern.

The speaker also needs to focus on one issue at a time as opposed to presenting several ideas, complaints, or issues at once. This helps to decrease the information that has to be processed by the listener. As a rule of thumb, statements of concern that are longer than six or seven sentences are usually problematic for listeners. The therapist can help the partners condense and shorten their expressions to more manageable units by helping the couple to summarize their concerns. Since many couples will quickly change subjects and digress into a variety of complaints during a single conversation, it is often necessary to help them focus on a single issue at a time.

The second step in communication training follows the careful practice of successful speaking and listening. This step emphasizes the importance of *demonstrating understanding* to one's partner. Important skills in this step include such behaviors as paraphrasing or restatements. Paraphrasing is the restatement of the essential elements of a message received from one's partner. This can be accomplished by having the listening spouse simply restate what the other partner has just said. The idea is to identify the main elements of the partner's message. One other way to approach the task is to ask the listener to first reflect the content of the other partner's message, then to identify the underlying emotion that is being expressed. The restatement is essentially a way of demonstrating understanding between partners. The demonstration of understanding is most important in showing respect for the partner's ideas and seems very necessary in establishing a cooperative environment between partners.

Once the message of the original speaker has been received and paraphrased by the listener, the speaker either indicates that the paraphrase was accurate or clarifies the intent of the original message. In this manner the first message can be sent, received, and paraphrased until it has been accurately understood.

Step three is the exchange of roles for speaker and listener. The listener now becomes the speaker and the first speaker is now the listener. The process of speaking, listening, paraphrasing, and correcting then proceeds as before until both partners are satisfied that they have been understood.

One of the most beneficial features of these communication skills is the *slow down* effect they have on a couple's interaction. The process of slowing down interaction has several positive results. First, it increases the probability of understanding by decreasing the volume of information that must be processed by each partner. Second, it decreases the probability of accelerating negative and coercive cycles that are typical of distressed couples. And, if nothing else, it helps couples to slow down their runaway interaction patterns and can help in decreasing their negative interaction pattern.

Problem Solving

Problem solving follows paraphrasing and answers the question of what to do when both partners understand each other but don't necessarily agree with what has been said, or don't share their partner's concern.

In this case it is useful to teach a solution-focused problem-solving process. There are at least two versions of problem solving. The first is a direct negotiation method. In this method, one partner asks for a change in the other partner's actions. The request should be specific, should focus on behavior, and preferably should identify something that can be done more frequently. After hearing the request, the listener briefly paraphrases the request and either (1) agrees to do what is asked or (2) offers a compromise solution to the request. If a solution has been reached at this point, the negotiation ends and the agreement is written. If the negotiation proceeds, the original speaker is now in a position to accept the compromise, or offer an additional compromise solution. If the original recipient of the request agrees, the negotiation ends and the agreement is recorded. If no agreement is reached by this point, the negotiation is unlikely to be concluded with this method. Instead, the second form of problem solving might be used.

The second method is more complicated, but teaches a wider range of skills. It involves a structured set of specific steps, which include identifying the problem, discussing one problem at a time, focusing on present events, emphasizing behavior rather than attitudes or personality characteristics, accepting responsibility for one's own part in the problem, brainstorming solutions, discussing the brainstorm ideas, and selecting alternatives.

Identifying the problem is done by having both partners identify an area they would like to discuss. The therapist helps frame the problem description as one of mutual concern or disagreement. Examples might be, "We disagree about how to spend our money" (rather than "You are selfish with the money") or "We need to spend more time together" or "We do not show appreciation to one another frequently enough." In these examples, the couples would be guided to identify each problem as a mutual problem, not one of the faults or deficiencies of either partner.

Discussing one problem at a time helps limit the amount of sidetracking into other issues. Changing subjects can be quite distracting for couples' discussions and can lead to a whole series of unrelated discussions that impede understanding of the issue at hand. This does not mean that the related issues are unimportant; they are important. Rather, it means that they will be discussed in turn.

It is often necessary to have the couple *take turns* in raising issues and concerns. This helps to balance the therapist's attention equally on the concerns of each.

Focusing on present events is necessary in helping couples discuss the here and now of their concerns rather than debate the merits of each person's case, recollections of past events, or accuracy in reporting these events to the therapist. The focus is on helping the couple identify their immediate concerns about their ongoing relationship issues.

The *emphasis of these discussions should be on the behavior* of concern, rather than attitudes, perceived intentions, or personality characteristics of either partner. This principle encourages discussion that guides couples away from the personal attacks and retaliations that are typical of distressed couples' interactions. Instead, the focus is on more manageable issues that can be identified in a less personalized manner.

Accepting responsibility for one's own part in the problem helps to deescalate the typical blaming and counterblaming cycles of distressed couples. When one person acknowledges his or her own role in the problem, the other partner is often less likely to react defensively to that person's concern. Examples of accepting responsibility are "I know that when I am angry with the children, it scares you" or "I know I have not been handling the money very well lately."

The next step in problem solving is for the couple to *brainstorm* solutions—that is, to identify as many solutions as possible in an atmosphere of acceptance. These solutions are to be identified and recorded, but not evaluated at this point. The principle is that the more freely couples generate solutions, the more likely they are to produce one or more solutions that are both effective and mutually agreeable. Early evaluation of solutions often leads to a decrease in the number and quality of the solutions generated.

Discussing the brainstorm ideas follows. In this step the couple is free to discuss, dismiss, and establish priorities for their possible alternatives. This is the task of cutting down the list of alternatives by first removing the impossible, the ridiculous, and the impractical. This judgment is left to the couple, with both partners having veto power over any of the suggested alternatives. This balances power in the relationship and emphasizes the importance of cooperation and agreement in the joint problem-solving activity.

Finally, after the alternatives are evaluated, the couple is asked to *select alternatives* from among those generated. The selection process should emphasize give-and-take from each partner and should include specific and clear communication about what each partner will do to help solve the problem.

Contracting

Contracting may follow problem-solving and negotiation training for couples. The idea is to develop a set of agreements regarding specific changes in behavior that each spouse will engage in. Each spouse will commit to make changes in behavior after such changes have been requested and negotiated.

There are several versions of contracting. Early in the development of behavioral marital therapy, contracts were quid pro quo agreements that specified changes by each partner in a tit-for-tat exchange contract structure. In many cases, the contract would also specify rewards or mild punishments that would follow the desired change or lack of effort. This form of contract may be appropriate in some cases, but has not been found to be particularly helpful in many others. The reasons are twofold. First, such contracts are often perceived as coercive in nature. Spouses are asked to engage in behavior that they may have serious reservations about, but they may feel compelled to agree. In general, agreement to change behavior can be developed, but only after the negative assumptions about the other have been reduced to the point that couples can assume a degree of collaboration and mutual respect. Attempts to force behavior change through the development of contracts can lead to increased couple conflict and early termination of therapy.

Second, partners in distressed relationships are often highly reactive to any perceived lack of effort, disinterest, or perceived dishonesty on their partner's part. As a result, the changes agreed to in a contract are not likely to occur fast enough to suit either spouse. Instead, spouses intently watch their partner for any sign of not fulfilling the agreement, fulfilling the agreement imperfectly or incompletely, backsliding, or making mistakes in fulfilling the agreement. If such an event is perceived, they then usually disqualify the entire agreement and launch into a series of recriminations directed toward their partner. This often can result in serious escalations of couple conflict.

Another form of contract has been the good faith model. In this paradigm, the agreements to change are made, but no specific positive or negative consequences are developed. The idea is that once couples understand what change is desired, they will then proceed to make the changes necessary without any specific reward for doing so.

The major advantage of the good faith agreements is that they are efficient and easy to use. Therapists can quickly guide the couple through a discussion about what is wanted. These requests for change can be translated into the objective and observable behavior that is the basis of most contracts. The final step is to have both spouses agree to make the changes specified. The requirement, of course, is that they make this agreement in good faith, with a willingness to change, without reference to their partner's behavior.

The major disadvantage of such contracts is that they assume a great deal about the couple. First, they assume that both partners are willing to change without any explicit reference to their partner's behavior. This assumption is often not met in highly distressed couples since each partner tends to be highly reactive to the other partner. Second, they assume that the couple has already developed a level of cooperation and trust that enables them to freely discuss their concerns, and have some expectation that their partner will respect and respond to their concerns. However, good faith contracts can be useful in later stages of therapy when the assumptions about trust and commitment have been met.

Increasing Positive Behavior

Simple behavior exchange agreements can add a degree of positive experience to a couple's relationship. These agreements can be quite useful in producing positive changes at home. First the focus is on identifying what each spouse would like from the partner and, second, on developing agreements to begin such changes. The goal of this procedure is to simultaneously increase positive behavior by each spouse toward the other. These agreements differ from contracts or other agreements developed in problem-solving sessions by the absence of an extended formal process to develop them. Instead, in a manner similar to good faith contracts, they are developed when an atmosphere of good intentions between partners is present.

At least two strategies can be used. First, for more mildly distressed cases, simply have each partner make specific requests of the other for more of a certain behavior. For example, Val says to Dave, "I would like you to spend more time with me in the evenings." Dave responds with "Okay, I can do that." Later, Dave is free to ask for something, such as "I would like more compliments about my exercise program." Val would then respond with "I can do that." In both examples, spouses are free to ask for something they would like more of, and the atmosphere is one where agreement to cooperate is likely.

In more distressed cases, one can ask both partners to specify what they are willing to volunteer to do. They are asked to think about things that their partner appreciates, and to do more of them. For example, Frank would identify awareness that Beth would like him to come home more promptly from work. He could volunteer to "be home by six each evening." Beth knows that Frank would like her to spend more time helping the children with homework. She could volunteer to "work each evening from seven to eight with the kids." In both examples, the partner volunteering the actions decides what he or she wishes to volunteer. There is not a clearly identified reciprocal or linked agreement (when one partner's behavior is contingent on the other's). Rather, the agreement is for the good of the relationship, to "give it some gas."

Building Positives

Distressed couples often suffer from a scarcity of positive interactions of almost any kind. Consequently, other attempts at building more positives can be helpful. Spouses can be coached to do the following:

1. Discuss things they admire about their partner
2. Give praise
3. Discuss shared goals and aspirations for the future

4. Praise their partner to friends and family

5. Genuinely compliment the other's accomplish-ments and positive characteristics

6. Express affection toward each other in a noncon-tingent manner

7. Volunteer to do things the other partner likes without discussion (or thought) of getting some-thing in return

8. Give random and senseless acts of kindness

Soothing

Gottman (1994a, 1994b) emphasizes the importance of *flooding* during conflict. Flooding refers to an intense and diffuse state of physiological arousal accompanied by a sense of being overwhelmed, surprised, and disorganized by the partner's negative emotions. This flooding often is accompanied by a sense of disorientation and being shut down in one's ability to function constructively. Flooding can be an important process in the decline of marital sat-isfaction over time.

The direct opposite of the intense physiological arousal that occurs with flooding is a sense of calmness and con-trol. Hence the concept of soothing the couple during con-flict can be important. This is designed to slow down the interaction process to a safer and more manageable level as well as to counter the physiological effects of flooding. Since distressed couples are likely to reciprocate per-ceived negative behavior very quickly, the goal is to in-crease their ability to maintain control during conflict by calming down.

The first step is to help the couple recognize when a person is being overwhelmed by negative emotion. The emotional experience can often be identified by a general state of increased physiological arousal. This state is ac-companied by increased heart rate, respiration, and gen-eral "system overload." The therapist can identify high levels of emotional arousal by observing the nonverbal signals associated with emotional arousal. For example, breathing rates, face flushing, general agitation, constricting of the muscles in the face, neck, or hands can be observed quite readily. These may be clues to an increased level of emotional and physiological arousal.

Next both partners need to make a deliberate effort to calm themselves down. Often, the couple can agree on a strategy to provide soothing for themselves and possibly for each other. These can include time out from interaction, taking a break, or just relaxing before discussion continues.

Soothing can also be accomplished by "self-talk" strategies such as repeating the following key phrases:

- "This is not the end of the world."
- "We are going to be okay; this is just a tough time right now."
- "This is not personal."
- "I can handle this."
- "This is basically a good marriage; we are just trying to work things out right now."
- "I may not agree, but I can appreciate her (his) point of view."

Calming down is especially important for men since they are more likely to be overwhelmed through physiological arousal during conflict (Gottman, 1994a). The key is often for the wife to accept the idea of a calming down period, since she is more likely to be conflict engaging and may not understand the necessity of such breaks. Requesting a break can be quite uncomfortable and artificial at first, but it will become more natural after it has been done frequently.

Nonverbal Skills

Nonverbal communication is an important means of information exchange. Two classes of nonverbal skill are most important. First, there is the ability to use nonverbal behavior to demonstrate accurate tracking of one's partner's communication or, in other words, paying attention and responding appropriately when one's spouse is speaking. Appropriate nonverbal behavior includes maintaining eye contact, nodding the head, smiling when appropriate, and maintaining a neutral or positive facial expression.

Inappropriate behaviors include failing to make eye contact during discussion, looking away excessively, and allowing facial expressions of disgust, contempt, or disdain when disagreeing with what is being said (Gottman, 1994a, 1994b). Examples include rolling eyes, pursing lips, frowning, or sarcastic smiling.

Second, body language skills are important in demonstrating emotional engagement, empathy, tracking, and understanding. These include maintaining close physical proximity to one's partner during discussion and leaning forward toward the spouse, but not in an intimidating or domineering manner. Additionally, spouses should keep an open body position with one another (e.g., arms to side or slightly in front, legs crossed at ankles but not at knees, etc.).

Partners should also learn to recognize their spouse's nonverbal behavior and facial expressions. This will allow them to identify their partner's physiological arousal level as well as the emotion that the partner may be experiencing. Particular attention should be paid to the nonverbal behavior associated with intense physiological arousal such as blushing, increased respiration, and agitation.

Demonstrating Empathy

This skill refers to the ability of both partners to identify and understand their partner's emotions and experiences. It does not mean agreeing with their partner's ideas or feelings; rather, it is the ability to identify, understand, and *demonstrate that understanding* to their partner.

Several previously mentioned verbal and nonverbal skills are important in exhibiting empathy. First, spouses should be able to track each other well. This skill demonstrates paying attention to what is being said. Second, they should be able to paraphrase or express back to their partner what they understand the problem to be. Third, they should be able to show some degree of acceptance of their partner's emotional experience. For example, a spouse might say, "I can see how this is important to you." Fourth, spouses should not try to talk their partner out of their concerns or dismiss their opinions, ideas, or feelings.

Talking About Emotions

Asking couples to express their feelings and emotions helps the spouses understand one another at a different and potentially deeper level than does normal conversation. Emotional expression differs from normal conversation in that it reveals information about more deeply felt emotions than is usually shared on a day-to-day basis.

The therapist facilitates the process of talking about emotions by first teaching *the language of emotion*. This may include the vocabulary of emotion as opposed to the vocabulary of thought. Put another way, some words describe emotions, while others identify and describe thought. Examples include "I feel sad" versus "I think this is sad"; "I am confused" versus "This is confusing"; and "I am angry" versus "This makes me mad."

Identifying emotions can be achieved by helping the spouses to identify and label their own internal emotional responses to current or recent events. In order to facilitate this process, the therapist may need to ask such questions as: "How do you feel when your partner says that?" "What is your greatest fear right now?" "What are you most nervous about right now?"

Partners will often seek to *deflect* such discussion to an intellectual level, or possibly to another topic, as a way of diffusing the emotional focus. In these cases the therapist needs to provide a degree of structure and control of the session by refocusing the spouse on the issues and experiences at hand. It may also be necessary to *set the stage* for discussing emotions by developing a safe environment in which spouses can express their emotions and potentially become more vulnerable to each other. There is almost no point in expecting couples to share their innermost feelings unless the therapeutic environment has established that such sharing and expression will be respected by the therapist and each spouse. Pushing for emotional expression without setting the stage may lead to greater anxiety and increase the potential for therapy dropouts (Allgood & Crane, 1991).

Next, the therapist *focuses* the spouses' attention on what they are experiencing "right now" in the therapy session, as problematic discussions are occurring. The goal is for couples to identify two levels of their own emotions, those they are consciously aware of but may be reluctant to share because of constraining beliefs or circumstances, and those they may not be aware of but that can be identified by therapist investigation and interpretation.

Finally, the spouses can learn to express those emotions constructively by expressing them directly to their partner. As these emotions are shared by the speaking spouse and respected by the listening spouse, greater emotional engagement is fostered.

Emphasize Progress

The therapist can often help the couple develop a sense of hope about their relationship and their prospects for therapy. This may be necessary since many distressed couples are likely to view their relationship in a very negative light. Feelings of hopelessness are also common since most couples do not enter therapy until their own attempts to influence their partner's behavior have been unsuccessful. In such cases, it is common for the spouses to have very low expectations about the likelihood of change occurring in therapy.

Although therapists cannot decide the outcome of therapy or the ultimate outcome of the marriage, they can provide some perspective to the couple. In many cases, couples respond to *normalization* ideas, that is, the idea that many couples experience these same difficulties and that most couples can improve their relationship by learning to understand one another better and by learning new skills.

Sometimes it is helpful to identify the common interaction problems of couples that can lead to distress. This information may help spouses understand that their problems are not unique and that they are not alone in what they are experiencing.

It may also be helpful to emphasize the progress being made in each session and between sessions. Pointing out what has been, is being, and can be done, and what can happen as a result of these efforts, may overcome a few of the fatalistic attitudes that some spouses hold.

Reframe

This means to help the spouses see their problems in new ways and eventually attach a more benign interpretation to their partner and their problems. The goals of reframing are to (1) remove the idea of individual deficit or fault; (2) attribute the problem to the relationship, rather than to the individuals involved; (3) assign a more positive connotation to the problem (e.g., this is a problem of misunderstanding each other rather than a problem of Mary's being distant from Bob); and, most importantly, (4) reframe the problem in a way that is *amenable to treatment* (Griffin, 1993, p. 26).

The goal of the therapist is to help make these cognitive shifts by discussing the problem from different angles, presenting the problem in different ways that identify the fault as being something other than one partner's terrible personality or malevolent intent. If the partners can accept a reinterpretation of the problem into a more benign form, they may decrease their blaming of one another and their negative perceptions of each other's meaning or motives.

The process of reframing the problem is one of subtle negotiation where the therapist gathers information, puts a new spin on the data and asks that the couple accept this new interpretation. Oftentimes, this process is negotiable as the therapist works toward a definition and description of the problem that the couple will accept. The final agreement always contains a description of the presenting problem that is benign and that is amenable to treatment (Griffin, 1993).

How to Deal with Unsolvable Problems

It is also important to discuss the inevitability that some problems are, in fact, unsolvable. It is not necessary for couples to agree about everything nor is it possible to negotiate and compromise about every disagreement or difference in a relationship. Some situations simply must be accepted as they are. For example, some characteristics of one's spouse are simply not likely to change. It is important that both persons learn to understand the other's point of view even if they do not agree with it. Also, spouses must identify for themselves which differences are acceptable and which are not. As discussed in Chapter 1, given the consequences of not accepting a difference and the possibility of pursuing a divorce or separation, spouses should consider this decision very carefully.

10

CLIENT RESISTANCE AND PERFORMANCE PROBLEMS

Resistance is a term that is often used to denote unwillingness to participate in therapy in a manner deemed necessary by the therapist. In such cases, the problem may be described as "one's conscious or unconscious psychological defense against bringing repressed (unconscious) thoughts to light" (American Psychiatric Association [APA], 1980, p. 119). However, in an interactionally based couple therapy model, resistance is seen as a natural response to a request for change. Resistance reflects the homeostatic nature of the couple's interactional system. In other words, the resistance to change lies in the interactional system, not in the unconscious or repressed psychological defenses of the individuals. For example, couples may resist spending more time together because doing so may lead to more conflict, not because either spouse has an unconscious need to remain distant from the other partner.

Taken in this way, it is important to understand the natural built-in difficulty that couples will face as they endeavor to change their tried-and-true interaction patterns. They will usually be reluctant to try, or they may say that such a change would be uncomfortable, unnatural, or artificial. Given the inherent difficulty in learning new ways of interacting, especially in such an emotionally charged environment, it would be naive to expect couples to respond with enthusiasm to each suggestion or assignment made by the therapist, no matter how well crafted the intervention.

Often, what might be taken as resistance can be seen as a problem in being able to perform a particular task or request. This definition of resistance is different from other ideas about the problem. Instead of looking for a psychological defense or an underlying repressed emotion, one should look for the errors in the intervention or treatment design that are blocking progress.

DEALING WITH RESISTANCE AND PERFORMANCE PROBLEMS

Concerns about change are to be expected, even predicted, when working with couples. *Anticipate them before they happen.* Foresee where problems are likely to develop and incorporate these issues into the therapy plan.

Background information about couples' interaction patterns, differences between distressed and nondistressed couples, and gender differences in couple interaction are especially important knowledge. In fact, the more one knows about marital interaction patterns in general, the more one can plan for those issues where change will be most difficult and where resistance will be most likely to emerge. For example, one can easily predict that for some men responding in an emotional way is difficult. The therapist can foresee this potential area of resistance by saying, "Tom, I know that this may be difficult to do, but would you tell Margaret how it makes you feel when she says that about you?"

Conversely, since some women are likely to be more conflict engaging than their husbands, the instruction to slow down or to accept a more structured interaction approach may appear to discount the seriousness of their views. This potential area of difficulty can be prevented by the therapist's saying something like, "Margaret, I know that this will seem slow and clumsy right now, but would you give Tom more time to tell you what he thinks or feels about this issue?" Anticipating areas of difficulty and providing interventions to overcome them can lead to much more effective therapy for couples.

Next, remember that the best way to get compliance with a task or instructions in therapy is to *make sure the steps are appropriate to the couple.* The best way to establish that the step is appropriate is with the expressed agreement and acknowledgment of the couple. The following process is often helpful in developing and implementing appropriate tasks for couples.

First, ask "Does this task (instruction, assignment, etc.) *make sense?*" If they agree that it does, then the chances of their following through with the assignment are greatly increased. If they do not both agree that the task seems to make sense, then it needs to be changed. The therapist should ask questions about what is wrong with the assignment, what it is missing, or why it doesn't fit with their expectations. Following this conversation, the assignment can be reformulated to suit the understanding and abilities of the couple.

After the task has been redesigned, the question "Does this make sense now?" should be asked again. The couple is more likely to implement the instruction if they believe that it will be helpful to them (Crane et al., 1986).

Second, ask if they are *willing* to do it: "Is this okay?" If they agree, then they have in fact agreed to make the change or implement the suggestion. They are also more likely to complete the task or assignment if they have agreed that it is understandable and acceptable to them.

Once the couple understands the assignment and is willing to do it, it is particularly important to discuss the *significance of following through* on the task. Spouses usually react quite poorly to situations in which their partner has agreed to do something, but doesn't do it. They may interpret such an event as a lack of commitment on their partner's part and respond in kind.

Third, if they have understood the assignment and agreed to do it, but don't, first *assume that the therapist has made some mistake.* This safeguard assigns responsibility for therapy assignment where it belongs—with the therapist—and prevents the common tendency to blame the couple's resistance for problems that occur. Always seek to determine if the assignment was too big or too difficult a task. The steps may be too large or the therapist may be asking the couple to do things that they don't want to do.

Fourth, if the problem is a mistake by the therapist, then *apologize* for the mistake. It is not the couple's fault if we ask them to do something that they cannot. Instead, take responsibility for the problem, reformat the assignment, and check again for their understanding and agreement to complete it.

Fifth, if the couple still fails to complete the assignment, ask about the meaning of the failure. Possible questions include: "Is there really a lack of interest in pursuing therapy? Are you both (or is one of you) not committed to therapy or even attempting to work things out? Is one of you waiting for the other person to make a change first, before making an effort? Is one of you waiting for the other person to do it 'right' first or do it perfectly before being willing to try?" In such cases, an open discussion about the meaning of the failure can be instructive.

COMMON TYPES OF RESISTANCE AND
HOW TO HANDLE EACH

The most common type of performance problem occurs when one or both partners are *not capable of performing the task under any circumstance.* They just don't know how to do it. In this case, the therapist selected a task that was unrealistic for this couple. Instead, the therapist should take a step back and design interventions that teach the missing elements first. For example, the couple may really have no knowledge about balancing checkbooks or debt management. Here, basic skills in mathematics and family financial issues need to be handled first. Another example might be one or both partners' really having no knowledge about human physiology or anatomy. In this instance, information about such matters needs to be provided before one can expect couples to resolve many of their sexual problems.

The second most common performance problem occurs when *the person (or couple) is capable of performing the task or behavior, but can't in the current situation.* The performance problem in this situation lies with the therapist, who has given an assignment or intervention without an adequate understanding of the context in which the problem is occurring. More information is needed before an appropriate assignment can be suggested. For example, therapists who are themselves childless may seriously underestimate the time and energy required by a client's children. The therapist may mistakenly prescribe assignments that are thus precluded by the couple's daily schedule. Hence the therapist needs to be certain that what is being asked can in fact be done in the current situation.

The third and most difficult type of performance problem occurs when *the person (or couple) is capable of the task, but won't do it in the current situation.* In this case, the problem lies with the person (or couple). The question now becomes "What is the root of the decision not to complete the task?" It may be that the therapist was wrong, that the assignment was not appropriate, that the steps were too large. On the other hand, it may also be that there are other reasons that the performance problem continues to occur. One possibility is that the spouses may not be recognizing their partner's efforts. This is a common problem when one partner attempts to change but the efforts go unrecognized and unrewarded. For example, the wife might be trying to engage her husband in more meaningful discussions, but the husband doesn't notice and doesn't respond to her efforts. The wife is likely to give up too soon, before her efforts have been in place long enough to be noticed.

Another possibility is that one partner is attempting to change, but the efforts are not acceptable to the other because they aren't being done perfectly. Continuing the above example, in this instance the complaining partner might say something like "I know he is trying to talk to me more, but he always does it just before we get into bed and I am too exhausted to even care."

A third possibility is that some partners will not recognize or appreciate their partner's attempts because they aren't doing them for the right reasons. Instead, they say that "they are only doing it because they have to." This belief puts their partners in a catch-22: if they do nothing they are not trying, but if they try, they are doing it for the wrong reasons. In both cases, the complaining partner is not allowing the other spouse any chance to change.

Under these circumstances, the therapist needs to address the importance of *recognizing effort* by identifying and commenting on the exertions of each spouse. For example, at the end of each session, it can be helpful to recognize instances where each spouse has been courageous or made noticeable efforts in the session. It is also possible to spend some time at the beginning of a session to review and discuss the efforts of the past week. Here, again, the therapist can set the example by focusing on the efforts that have been made.

Therapists can also recognize the problems inherent in *expecting perfection* from the couple. This can be done in several ways: first, by the therapist's not expecting perfection from the couple in the session; next, by anticipating and addressing the likely difficulties in performing perfectly at home as well.

Finally, there may be an unexpressed purpose behind the therapy. The most common example is one spouse who attends the sessions but who has already made another decision, usually to terminate the marriage, and wants the other partner in therapy when it happens. The therapist should begin by assuming that the couple is being honest in their statements about why they are seeking therapy. However, one should also be cognizant of the fact that all spouses are not honest in all cases. If the therapist has reason to doubt the veracity of the therapy goals, such suspicions should be addressed in a frank and candid manner. Overall, most problems of couples' resistance to therapeutic instructions or tasks can be conceptualized as problems in the partners' ability to do what has been asked. For the most part, the responsibility for the resistance lies with the therapist. Assignments need to be carefully designed to ensure that they suit the needs of each couple.

11

WHAT TO DO WITH SEVERELY DISTRESSED CASES

As discussed earlier in Chapter 3, there appear to be several key ingredients for successful marital therapy (Alexander et al., 1994). However, very little is known about how to effectively treat couples who are more than moderately distressed. Consequently, this chapter will discuss the ways in which more severely distressed couples can be identified and speculate about some possible strategies for treating these types of cases.

How to Identify More Severely Distressed Couples

One useful way to identify couples who are more severely distressed is to use one of the common marital satisfaction or stability measures as a pretreatment screening tool. Using one of these instruments will allow therapists to determine the status of the couple they are working with and to compare this couple with those who have been studied in the research literature.

Marital Quality Assessments

Marital Adjustment Test

The Marital Adjustment Test (MAT) (see Appendix A) assesses overall marital quality (Locke & Wallace, 1959). The MAT has been used extensively in clinical and nonclinical research. The instrument is internally consistent, and it has been demonstrated to successfully differentiate between distressed and nondistressed marital relationships (e.g., Birchler & Webb, 1977; Williams, 1979). The score on the MAT ranges from 2 to 158, with higher scores indicating greater marital satisfaction.

Dyadic Adjustment Scale and the Revised Dyadic Adjustment Scale

The Dyadic Adjustment Scale (DAS) (see Appendix B) is a measure of an individual's adjustment to marriage (Spanier, 1976). The total score on the DAS ranges from 0 to 151, with higher scores indicating greater marital adjustment or satisfaction. Spanier (1985) reports that the DAS has been used in over one thousand studies.

However, since some evidence (e.g., Crane, Busby, & Larson, 1991) suggests that problems of validity exist for some of the scales on the DAS, and in using this instrument for nondistressed couples (Crane et al., 1990), the Revised Dyadic Adjustment Scale (RDAS), has been developed (Busby et al., 1995). The RDAS (available from this author) has several advantages over the original DAS. First, it is shorter, with 14 instead of 32 items, thus allowing easier application in many settings. Second, three reliable subscales of Dyadic Consensus, Dyadic Satisfaction, and Dyadic Cohesion have been reformulated and have superior psychometric properties to the original DAS. Finally, the RDAS has been developed and tested using both distressed couples seeking marital therapy and volunteer nondistressed couples. Possible scores on the RDAS range from 0 to 69, with higher scores representing greater marital adjustment.

Interpreting the Marital Quality Scales

If a pretreatment assessment instrument, such as the MAT, DAS, or RDAS, is used, moderately distressed couples typically both score in the range of 60 to 100 on the MAT, 80 to 107 on the DAS (Crane et al., 1990), and 32 to 45 on the RDAS. Most studies of the outcome of marital therapy have used couples whose averaged MAT scores are about 82 on the MAT (Hahlweg & Markman, 1988). This MAT score can be translated to be about 96 on the DAS (Crane et al., 1990), and 41 on the RDAS.

More severe cases can be identified as one standard deviation (or more) below the mean for clinical couples presenting for marital therapy (Crane et al., 1990). This would mean couple average MAT scores of 60 or less, RDAS scores of 32 or less, and DAS scores of 80 or less. These kinds of cases are generally less available for research purposes, and less is known about appropriate treatments for them.

Marital Status Inventory

Scores on the Marital Status Inventory (MSI) (Appendix C) are also helpful in identifying more highly distressed couples (Weiss & Cerreto, 1980). The MSI is a 14-item true or false test that is designed to measure divorce potential. It measures the cognitive and behavioral steps toward divorce and has been found to be helpful in predicting divorce (Crane, Soderquist, & Frank, 1995; Crane, Soderquist, & Gardner, 1995; Newfield, 1985). Several studies (e.g., Crane & Mead, 1980; Crane, Newfield, & Armstrong, 1984; Weiss & Cerreto, 1980) have supported the MSI as a valid and reliable instrument. In general, wives' scores are more predictive of divorce than are husbands'. Couples in which the wife scores greater than seven on the MSI should be considered severely distressed and at high risk for divorce (Crane et al., 1984; Crane, Soderquist, & Frank, 1995).

Clinical Profiles of Distressed Couples

Highly distressed couples can often be identified by the degree to which they seem to fit the clinical profile of distressed couples discussed in Chapter 5. All distressed couples have these characteristics to a degree. However, the more distressed a couple is, the more prevalent the characteristics become.

In the interaction of highly distressed couples, the therapist can observe higher levels of negative emotion, coercive acts, and defensive behaviors along with a greater interpersonal distance between the partners than would be observed with moderately distressed couples. Also, conflict resolution is much more difficult for distressed couples. They are more negative and coercive toward their partner. In addition, conflict lasts longer and is more intense. These couples have little ability or proclivity to exit conflict cycles.

In addition, negative exchanges and punishing behaviors are delivered and reciprocated very quickly. Distressed couples exchange higher rates of negative behaviors over much shorter periods of time. That is, if a punishing behavior is directed from one partner to another, the victim is usually likely to reciprocate immediately with an equally negative behavior.

More highly distressed couples can also be identified by five main behavior clusters that distinguish distressed from nondistressed couples (Gottman, 1994a). These include criticism (e.g., attacking, blaming), contempt (e.g., name calling, sneering), defensiveness (e.g., denying responsibility, "yes-butting"), stonewalling (e.g., ignoring and withdrawal), and ruminating about negative aspects of their relationship. As mentioned previously, all distressed couples demonstrate these behavioral clusters to a degree. The more distressed the couple, the more the interaction between the partners is dominated by these features. However, according to Gottman (1994a), the presence of stonewalling is particularly important. This may be because it signals a general attitude of hopelessness and lack of investment in the relationship.

TREATMENT IDEAS FOR SEVERELY DISTRESSED COUPLES

Always be realistic with regards to what is known about treating these couples. It may be that couples in this degree of distress are not treatable with the current technology available. It may be that their concerns are so deep and so pervasive and that they are so conflicted as to be untreatable.

This does not mean that the therapist should discontinue therapy or recommend divorce or separation. Such decisions are the responsibility of the couple. Instead, being realistic about what is known may provide a guide to the therapist about what can and can not be reasonably expected from the couple.

Also, it may be true that therapy could help these couples to resolve their problems, but because they are not likely to volunteer for participation in a treatment outcome study offered at a university clinic, they have not been included in most studies. Hence, our knowledge about how to treat their concerns is quite limited.

In any event, clinical experience suggests that these cases are extremely difficult to treat. When treatment is successful it appears to have two key ingredients. First, the therapist sets small goals and is realistic about change and how fast it may occur. For example, couples may demand all-or-nothing changes from their partner, but the therapist can identify small steps that signify change. Instead of working on one partner's "choosing his family over me," the therapist can discuss ways to decide things together. The goal would be to help the couple begin to discuss problems and make decisions together, before tackling the potentially volatile issue of in-laws.

Part of working toward realistic goals is proceeding slowly: these couples generally need more time in therapy than their less distressed counterparts. Ironically, they may need more time in therapy than others but demand faster treatment. In these cases, more frequent meetings may be beneficial for the couple.

The second ingredient of successful therapy is that the therapist tries to change the couple's fundamental perceptions of each other. As was discussed earlier in treating moderately distressed couples, the therapist should focus first on establishing a collaborative set for therapy. This step is particularly important for more severely distressed couples since their interactions are usually extremely negative and even more coercive than those of many less distressed couples.

The basic principle is to enable the couple to ascribe their present difficulties to almost any source other than their partner's malevolent intent or diseased personality. Use reframes or any other device to help them make the cognitive shift from blaming to at least the rudiments of a less critical position toward their partner. Some good targets to blame might include unconsciously learned sex-role characteristics, dysfunctional families of origin, external pressures and events such as employment, or social problems. The choices are limitless, so search for the ideas or interpretations that the couple might accept. If they can agree that there may be more to their present concerns than their partner's bad intentions, they have taken the first step toward establishing a collaborative therapeutic relationship. Once blaming is decreased, more standard methods of treatment can be utilized.

One final important issue for therapists working with these couples is the possibility that the couple seeking marital therapy may have domestic violence as the main issue. Although these cases are difficult to identify because of the secrecy, shame, and potential legal issues associated with battery, the therapist should firmly inquire about this potentiality. If violence is present in the relationship, other treatment alternatives specifically designed for such couples should be pursued.

APPENDIX A

MARITAL ADJUSTMENT TEST*

Name ————————————————   Circle one: Male   Female

Date: ————————————   Score: ————————————

1. Check the dot on the scale line below that best describes the degree of happiness, everything considered, of your present marriage. The middle point, "happy," represents the
   degree of happiness which most people get from marriage, and the scale gradually ranges
   on one side to those few who are very unhappy in marriage and on the other, to those
   few who experience extreme joy or felicity in marriage.

   .   .   .   .

   _____

   Very   Happy   Perfectly
   unhappy   happy

---

*From "Short marital-adjustment and prediction tests: Their reliability and validity," by
H. J. Locke and K. M. Wallace, 1959, *Marriage and Family Living, 21,* pp. 251–255. Copyright 1959 by the National Council on Family Relations and Karl M. Wallace. Adapted
with permission.

State the approximate extent of agreement or disagreement between you and your mate on the following items. Please check each column.

	Always agree	Almost always agree	Occasionally disagree	Frequently disagree	Almost always disagree	Always disagree
2. Handling family finances						
3. Matters of recreation						
4. Demonstration of affection						
5. Friends						
6. Sex relations						
7. Conventionality (right, good, or proper conduct)						
8. Philosophy of life						
9. Ways of dealing with in-laws						

Please check the appropiate reply:

10. When disagreements arise, they usually result in:
    Husband giving in ☐   Wife giving in ☐   Agreement by mutual give and take ☐

11. Do you and your mate engage in outside interests together?
    All of them ☐   Some of them ☐   Very few of them ☐   None of them ☐

12. In leisure time do you generally prefer: to be "on the go?" ☐   to stay at home? ☐

    Does your mate generally prefer: to be "on the go?" ☐   to stay at home? ☐

13. Do you ever wish you had not married?
    Frequently ☐   Occasionally ☐   Rarely ☐   Never ☐

14. If you had your life to live over, do you think you would:
    Marry the same person ☐   Marry a different person ☐   Not marry at all ☐

15. Do you confide in your mate:
    Almost never ☐   Rarely ☐   In most things ☐   In everything ☐

MARITAL ADJUSTMENT TEST SCORING KEY*

Name _____   Circle one: Male   Female

Date: _____   Score: _____

1. Check the dot on the scale line below that best describes the degree of happiness, everything considered, of your present marriage. The middle point, "happy," represents the degree of happiness which most people get from marriage, and the scale gradually ranges on one side to those few who are very unhappy in marriage and on the other, to those few who experience extreme joy or felicity in marriage.

0	2	7	15	20	25	35
.	.	.	.	.	.	.

Very unhappy	Happy	Perfectly happy

---

*From "Short marital-adjustment and prediction tests: Their reliability and validity," by H. J. Locke and K. M. Wallace, 1959, *Marriage and Family Living, 21,* pp. 251–255. Copyright 1959 by the National Council on Family Relations and Karl M. Wallace. Adapted with permission.

State the approximate extent of agreement or disagreement between you and your mate on the following items. Please check each column.

	Always agree	Almost always agree	Occasionally disagree	Frequently disagree	Almost always disagree	Always disagree
2. Handling family finances	5	4	3	2	1	0
3. Matters of recreation	5	4	3	2	1	0
4. Demonstration of affection	8	6	4	2	1	0
5. Friends	5	4	3	2	1	0
6. Sex relations	15	12	9	4	1	0
7. Conventionality (right, good, or proper conduct)	5	4	3	2	1	0
8. Philosophy of life	5	4	3	2	1	0
9. Ways of dealing with in-laws	5	4	3	2	1	0

Please check the appropiate reply:

10. When disagreements arise, they usually result in:
    Husband giving in [0]   Wife giving in [2]   Agreement by mutual give and take [10]

11. Do you and your mate engage in outside interests together?
    All of them [10]   Some of them [8]   Very few of them [3]   None of them [0]

12. In leisure time do you generally prefer: to be "on the go?" ☐   to stay at home? ☐

    Does your mate generally prefer: to be "on the go?" ☐   to stay at home? ☐

    (Stay at home for both, 10 points; "on the go" for both, 3 points; disagreement, 2 points)

13. Do you ever wish you had not married?
    Frequently [0]   Occasionally [3]   Rarely [8]   Never [15]

14. If you had your life to live over, do you think you would:
    Marry the same person [15]   Marry a different person [0]   Not marry at all [1]

15. Do you confide in your mate:
    Almost never [0]   Rarely [2]   In most things [10]   In everything [10]

APPENDIX B

DYADIC ADJUSTMENT SCALE*

Sample Items

	Always agree	Almost always agree	Occasionally disagree	Frequently disagree	Almost always disagree	Always disagree
1. Handling family finances	___	___	___	___	___	___
2. Matters of recreation	___	___	___	___	___	___
3. Religious matters	___	___	___	___	___	___
4. Demonstrations of affection	___	___	___	___	___	___
5. Friends	___	___	___	___	___	___
6. Sex relations	___	___	___	___	___	___

DYADIC ADJUSTMENT SCALE SCORING KEY*

Sample Items

	Always agree	Almost always agree	Occasionally disagree	Frequently disagree	Almost always disagree	Always disagree
1. Handling family finances	5	4	3	2	1	0
2. Matters of recreation	5	4	3	2	1	0
3. Religious matters	5	4	3	2	1	0
4. Demonstrations of affection	5	4	3	2	1	0
5. Friends	5	4	3	2	1	0
6. Sex relations	5	4	3	2	1	0

APPENDIX C

MARITAL STATUS INVENTORY*

We would like to get an idea of how your marriage stands right now. Please answer the following questions by checking true or false for each item.

True   *False*

_____   _____   1. I have occasionally thought of divorce or wished that I were separated from my spouse, usually after an argument or other incident.

_____   _____   2. I have considered a divorce or separation a few times other than during or shortly after a fight, although only in vague terms.

_____   _____   3. I have thought specifically about divorce or separation; I have considered who would get the kids, how things would be divided, and the pros and cons of such actions.

_____   _____   4. I have discussed the question of my divorce or separation with someone other than my spouse (trusted friend, psychologists, minister, etc.).

*From "The Marital Status Inventory: Development of a measure of dissolution potential," by R. L. Weiss and M. Cerreto, 1980, *The American Journal of Family Therapy, 8*, pp. 80–86. Copyright 1980 by Brunner/Mazel Publishers and R. L. Weiss. Adapted with permission.

———— ———— 5. I have not suggested to my spouse that I wished to be divorced or separated from him/her.

———— ———— 6. I have not made any specific plans to discuss separation or divorce with my spouse. I have not considered what I would say.

———— ———— 7. I have not discussed the issue seriously or at length with my spouse.

———— ———— 8. My spouse and I have separated. (This is a ( ) trial separation or ( ) permanent separation; check one.)

———— ———— 9. Thoughts of divorce occur to me very frequently, as often as once a week or more.

———— ———— 10. I have made no inquiries to non-professionals as to how long it takes to get a divorce, grounds for divorce, or costs involved in such action.

———— ———— 11. I have not consulted a lawyer or other legal aide about the matter.

———— ———— 12. I have set up an independent bank account in my name as a measure of protecting my own interests.

———— ———— 13. I have not contacted a lawyer to make preliminary plans for a divorce.

———— ———— 14. I have filed for divorce, or I am divorced.

MARITAL STATUS INVENTORY SCORING KEY*

We would like to get an idea of how your marriage stands right now. Please answer the following questions by checking true or false for each item.

True   *False*

True	False	
T		1. I have occasionally thought of divorce or wished that I were separated from my spouse, usually after an argument or other incident.
T		2. I have considered a divorce or separation a few times other than during or shortly after a fight, although only in vague terms.
T		3. I have thought specifically about divorce or separation; I have considered who would get the kids, how things would be divided, and the pros and cons of such actions.
T		4. I have discussed the question of my divorce or separation with someone other than my spouse (trusted friend, psychologists, minister, etc.).
	F	5. I have not suggested to my spouse that I wished to be divorced or separated from him/her.
	F	6. I have not made any specific plans to discuss separation or divorce with my spouse. I have not considered what I would say.

*From "The Marital Status Inventory: Development of a measure of dissolution potential," by R. L. Weiss and M. Cerreto, 1980, *The American Journal of Family Therapy, 8,* pp. 80–86. Copyright 1980 by Brunner/Mazel Publishers and R. L. Weiss. Adapted with permission.

_____	F	7. I have not discussed the issue seriously or at length with my spouse.
T	____	8. My spouse and I have separated. (This is a ( ) trial separation or ( ) permanent separation; check one.)
T	____	9. Thoughts of divorce occur to me very frequently, as often as once a week or more.
_____	F	10. I have made no inquiries to nonprofessionals as to how long it takes to get a divorce, grounds for divorce, or costs involved in such action.
_____	F	11. I have not consulted a lawyer or other legal aide about the matter.
T	____	12. I have set up an independent bank account in my name as a measure of protecting my own interests.
_____	F	13. I have not contacted a lawyer to make preliminary plans for a divorce.
T	____	14. I have filed for divorce, or I am divorced.

Score one point for each question answered in agreement with the indicated response. Higher scores are more predictive of divorce outcome, especially for women.

ADDITIONAL READINGS

As one becomes more familiar with the basic issues of marital therapy, a greater understanding of particular theoretical approaches can be helpful in expanding the therapist's ability to work with couples. The following list will guide the reader to important additional resources. Books and articles about specific theoretical approaches are presented first. Readings that focus on special problems and issues in couple therapy are offered next.

THEORY-SPECIFIC MODELS OF COUPLE THERAPY

Adlerian

Kern, R. M., Hawes, E. C., & Christensen, O. C. (Eds.). (1989). *Couples therapy: An Adlerian perspective.* Minneapolis, MN: Educational Media Corp.

Behavioral

Baucom, D. H., & Epstein, N. (1990). *Cognitive behavioral marital therapy.* New York: Brunner/Mazel.

Jacobson, N. S., & Margolin, G. (1979). *Marital therapy: Strategies based on social learning and behavior exchange principles.* New York: Brunner/Mazel.

Liberman, R. P., Wheeler, E. C., de Visser, L. A. J. M., Kuehnel, J., & Kuehnel, T. (1980). *The handbook of marital therapy: A positive approach to helping troubled relationships.* New York: Plenum.

Stuart, R. B. (1980). *Helping couples change: A social learning approach to marital therapy.* New York: Guilford.

Developmental

Bader, E., & Pearson, P. T. (1988). *In quest of the mythical mate: A developmental approach to diagnosis and treatment in couples therapy.* New York: Brunner/Mazel.

Existential/Experiential

Charny, I. W. (1992). *Existential–dialectical marital therapy: Breaking the secret code of marriage.* New York: Brunner/Mazel.

Emotionally Focused

Greenberg, L. S., & Johnson, S. M. (1988). *Emotionally focused therapy for couples.* New York: Guilford.

Ericksonian

Kershaw, C. J. (1992). *The couple's hypnotic dance: Creating Ericksonian strategies in marital therapy.* New York: Brunner/Mazel.

Intergenerational

Framo, J. L. (1982). *Explorations in marital and family therapy: Selected papers of James L. Framo.* New York: Springer.

Object Relations

Scharff, D. E., & Scharff, J. S. (1991). *Object relations couple therapy.* Northvale, NJ: Jason Aronson.

Psychodynamic

Lachkar, J. (1992). *The narcissistic/borderline couple: A psychoanalytic perspective on marital treatment.* New York: Brunner/Mazel.

Strean, H. S. (1985). *Resolving marital conflicts: A psychodynamic perspective.* New York: Wiley.

COMPARING DIFFERENT APPROACHES

Chasin, R., Grunebaum, H., & Herzig, M. (Eds.). (1990). *One couple, four realities: Multiple perspectives on couple therapy.* New York: Guilford.

Paolino, T. J., & McCrady, B. S. (Eds.). (1978). *Marriage and marital therapy: Psychoanalytic, behavioral, and systems theory perspectives.* New York: Brunner/Mazel.

Segraves, R. T. (1982). *Marital therapy: A combined psychodynamic–behavioral approach.* New York: Plenum.

OTHER MODELS OF COUPLE THERAPY

Guerin, P. J., Fay, L. F., Burden, S. L., & Kautto, J. G. (1987). *The evaluation and treatment of marital conflict: A four stage approach.* New York: Basic Books.

Nichols, W. C. (1988). *Marital therapy: An integrative approach.* New York: Guilford.

Waring, E. M. (1987). *Enhancing marital intimacy through facilitating cognitive self-disclosure.* New York: Brunner/Mazel.

Weeks, G. R. (Ed.). (1989). *Treating couples: The intersystem model of the Marriage Council of Philadelphia.* New York: Brunner/Mazel.

SPECIALIZED PROBLEMS AND ISSUES IN COUPLE THERAPY

Aging

Wolinsky, M. A. (1990). *A heart of wisdom: Marital counseling with older and elderly couples.* New York: Brunner/Mazel.

Assessment and Measurement

Fredman, N., & Sherman, R. (1987). *Handbook of measurements for marriage and family therapy.* New York: Brunner/Mazel.

Hiebert, W. J., Gillespie, J. P., & Stahmann, R. F. (1993). *Dynamic assessment in couple therapy.* New York: Lexington Books/Macmillan.

O'Leary, K. D. (Ed.). (1987). *Assessment of marital discord: An integration for research and clinical practice.* Hillsdale, NY: Lawrence Erlbaum.

Touliatos, J., Perlmutter, B. F., & Straus, M. A. (1990). *Handbook of family measurement techniques.* Newbury Park, CA: Sage.

Christian/Religious Focused

Del Vecchio, A., & Del Vecchio, M. (1980). *Preparing for the sacrament of marriage.* Notre Dame, IN: Ave Maria Press.

Grant, B. W. (1986). *Reclaiming the dream: Marriage counseling in the parish context.* Nashville, TN: Abingdon.

Worthington, E. L., Jr. (1989). *Marriage counseling: A Christian approach to counseling couples.* Downers Grove, IL: Inter-Varsity.

Domestic Violence

Ammerman, R. T., & Hersen, M. (1990). *Treatment of family violence: A source book.* New York: Wiley.

Busby, D. M. (Ed.). (1996). *The impact of violence on the family: Treatment approaches for therapists and other professionals working with families.* Needham Heights, MA: Allyn & Bacon.

Neidig, P. H., & Friedman, D. H. (1984). *Spouse abuse: A treatment program for couples.* Champaign, IL: Research Press.

Divorce Mediation

Haynes, J. M. (1981). *Divorce mediation: A practical guide for therapists and counselors.* New York: Springer.

Ethnicity

Ho, M. K. (1990). *Intermarried couples in therapy.* Springfield, IL: Charles C. Thomas.

Financial Issues

Poduska, B. E. (1993). *For love and money: A guide to finances and relationships.* Belmont, CA: Brooks/Cole.

Gender Issues

Bograd, M. (Ed.). (1991). *Feminist approaches for men in family therapy.* New York: Haworth Press.

Fitzpatrick, M. A. (1988). *Between husbands and wives: Communication in marriage.* Newbury Park, CA: Sage.

Group Therapy Approaches

Coche, J., & Coche, E. (1990). *Couples group psychotherapy: A clinical practice model.* New York: Brunner/Mazel.

Premarital and Remarital Issues

Stahmann, R. F., & Hiebert, W. J. (1987). *Premarital counseling: The professional's handbook* (2nd ed.). Lexington, MA: Lexington Books.

Marriage Enrichment

Hof, L., & Miller, W. (1981). *Marriage enrichment: Philosophy* process & program. Bowie, MD: R. J. Brady.

Mace, D., & Mace, V. (1983). *How to have a happy marriage: A step-by-step guide to an enriched relationship.* Nashville, TN: Abingdon.

Sex Therapy

Leiblum, S. R., & Rosen, R. C. (Eds.). (1989). *Principles and practice of sex therapy.* New York: Guilford.

Weeks, G. R., & Hof, L. (1987). *Integrating sex and marital therapy.* New York: Brunner/Mazel.

COLLECTIONS ABOUT PROBLEMS AND ISSUES IN COUPLE THERAPY

Gurman, A. S. (Ed.). (1985). *Casebook of marital therapy.* New York: Guilford.

Hughes, M. (1991). *Marriage counseling: An essential guide.* New York: Continuum.

Humphrey, F. G. (1983). *Marital therapy.* Englewood Cliffs, NJ: Prentice-Hall.

Jacobson, N. S., & Gurman, A. S. (Eds.). (1995). *Clinical handbook of couple therapy.* New York: Guilford.

Sherman, R., & Fredman, N. (1986). *Handbook of structured techniques in marriage and family therapy.* New York: Brunner/Mazel.

Sholevar, G. P. (Ed.). (1981). *The handbook of marriage and marital therapy.* Jamaica, NY: Spectrum.

Stahmann, R. F., & Hiebert, W. J. (1984). *Counseling in marital and sexual problems: A clinician's handbook* (3rd ed.). Lexington, MA: D. C. Heath.

Selected Research Reviews and Summary Articles

Alexander, J. F., Holtzworth-Munroe, A., & Jameson, P. (1994). The process and outcome of marriage and family therapy: Research review and evaluation. In A. E. Bergin & S. L. Garfield (Eds.), *Handbook of Psychotherapy and Behavior Change* (4th ed., pp. 595–630). New York: Wiley.

Gurman, A. S., Kniskern, D. P., & Pinsof, W. M. (1986). Research on the process and outcome of marital and family therapy. In A. E. Bergin & S. L. Garfield (Eds.), *Handbook of psychotherapy and behavior change* (3rd ed., pp. 565–626). New York: Wiley.

Jacobson, N. S., & Addis, M. E. (1993). Research on couples and couple's therapy: What do we know? Where are we going? *Journal of Consulting and Clinical Psychology, 61*, 85–93.

REFERENCES

Alexander, J. F., Holtzworth-Munroe, A., & Jameson, P. B. (1994). The process and outcome of marriage and family therapy: Research review and evaluation. In A. E. Bergin & S. L. Garfield (Eds.), *Handbook of psychotherapy and behavior change* (4th ed., pp. 595–630). New York: Wiley.

Allgood, S. M., & Crane, D. R. (1991). Predicting marital therapy dropouts. *Journal of Marital and Family Therapy, 17*, 73–79.

Amato, P. R., & Booth, A. (1991). Consequences of parental divorce and marital unhappiness for adult well-being. *Social Forces, 69*, 895–914.

Amato, P. R., & Keith, B. (1991). Parental divorce and the well-being of children: A meta-analysis. *Psychological Bulletin, 110*, 26–46.

American Association for Marriage and Family Therapy. (1991). *AAMFT code of ethics.* Washington, DC: Author.

American Psychiatric Association. (1980). *A psychiatric glossary* (5th ed.). Boston: Little, Brown.

Baucom, D. H., & Epstein, N. (1990). *Cognitive-behavioral marital therapy.* New York: Brunner/Mazel.

Baucom, D. H., & Hoffman, J. A. (1986). The effectiveness of marital therapy: Current status and application to the clinical setting. In N. S. Jacobson & A. Gurman (Eds.), *Clinical handbook of marital therapy* (pp. 597–620). New York: Guilford.

Bean, R. A., & Crane, D. R. (1996). Marriage and family therapy research with ethnic minorities: Current status. *The American Journal of Family Therapy, 24*, 3–8.

Beck, A. (1988). *Love is never enough.* New York: Harper & Row.

Birchler, G. R., & Webb, L. J. (1977). Discriminating interaction behaviors in happy and unhappy marriages. *Journal of Consulting and Clinical Psychology, 45*, 494–495.

Booth, A., & Edwards, J. N. (1989). Transmission of marital and family quality over the generations: The effect of parental divorce and unhappiness. *Journal of Divorce, 13*(1-2), 41–58.

Busby, D. M., Crane, D. R., Larson, J. H., & Christensen, C. (1995). A revision of the Dyadic Adjustment Scale for use with distressed and nondistressed couples: Construction Hierarchy and multidimensional scales. *Journal of Marital and Family Therapy, 21*, 289–308.

Cherlin, A. J. (1992). *Marriage, divorce, remarriage.* Cambridge, MA: Harvard University Press.

Clark, R. (1990). Economic dependency and divorce: Implications for the private sphere. *International Journal of Sociology of the Family, 20*(1), 47–65.

Coleman, M., & Ganong, L. H. (1992). Financial responsibility for children following divorce and remarriage. *Journal of Family and Economic Issues, 13*, 445–455.

Crane, D. R., Allgood, S. M., Larson, J. H., & Griffin, W. (1990). Assessing marital quality with distressed and nondistressed couples: A comparison and equivalency table for three frequently used measures. *Journal of Marriage and the Family, 52*, 87–93.

Crane, D. R., Busby, D. M., & Larson, J. H. (1991). A factor analysis of the Dyadic Adjustment Scale with distressed and nondistressed couples. *The American Journal of Family Therapy, 19*, 60–66.

Crane, D. R., Dollahite, D. C., Griffin, W., & Taylor, V. L. (1987). Diagnosing relationships with spatial distance: An empirical test of a clinical principle. *Journal of Marital and Family Therapy, 13*, 307–310.

Crane, D. R., & Griffin, W. (1983). Personal space: An objective measure of marital quality. *Journal of Marital and Family Therapy, 9*, 325–327.

Crane, D. R., Griffin, W., & Hill, R. D. (1986). Influence of therapist skills on client perceptions of marriage and family therapy outcome: Implications for supervision. *Journal of Marital and Family Therapy, 12*, 91–96.

Crane, D. R., & Mead, D. E. (1980). The Marital Status Inventory: Some preliminary data on an instrument to measure marital dissolution potential. *The American Journal of Family Therapy, 8*, 31–35.

Crane, D. R., Newfield, N., & Armstrong, D. (1984). Predicting divorce at marital therapy intake: Wives' distress and the Marital Status Inventory. *Journal of Marital and Family Therapy, 10*, 305–312.

Crane, D. R., Soderquist, J. N., & Frank, R. L. (1995). Predicting divorce at marital therapy intake: A preliminary model. *The American Journal of Family Therapy, 23*, 227–236.

Crane, D. R., Soderquist, J. N., & Gardner, M. D. (1995). Gender differences in the cognitive and behavioral steps towards divorce. *The American Journal of Family Therapy, 23*, 99–105.

Dadds, M. R., Schwartz, S., & Sanders, M. R. (1987). Marital discord and treatment outcome in behavioral treatment of child conduct disorders. *Journal of Consulting and Clinical Psychology, 55*, 396–403.

Finnie, R. (1993). Women, men, and the economic consequences of divorce: Evidence from Canadian longitudinal data. *The Canadian Review of Sociology and Anthropology, 30*, 205–241.

Funder, K. (1992). Australia: A proposal for reform. In L. J. Weitzman & M. Maclean (Eds.), *Economic consequences of divorce: The international perspective* (pp. 143–162). New York: Oxford.

Garfield, S. L. (1994). Research on client variables in psychotherapy. In A. E. Bergin & S. L. Garfield (Eds.), *Handbook of psychotherapy and behavior change* (4th ed., pp. 190–228). New York: Wiley.

Garfinkel, I. (1992). Child-support trends in the United States. In L. J. Weitzman & M. Maclean (Eds.), *Economic consequences of divorce: The international perspective* (pp. 205–218). New York: Oxford University Press.

Gately, D., & Schwebel, A. I. (1992). Favorable outcomes in children after parental divorce. *Journal of Divorce and Remarriage, 18*(3-4), 79–91.

Goode, W. J. (1992). World changes in divorce patterns. In L. J. Weitzman & M. Maclean (Eds.), *Economic consequences of divorce: The international perspective* (pp. 11–52). New York: Oxford.

Gottman, J. M. (1994a). *What predicts divorce?: The relationship between marital processes and marital outcomes.* Hillsdale, NJ: Lawrence Erlbaum.

Gottman, J. M. (1994b). *Why marriages succeed or fail.* New York: Simon and Schuster.

Gottman, J. M., & Krokoff, L. (1989). Marital interaction and marital satisfaction: A longitudinal view. *Journal of Consulting and Clinical Psychology, 57,* 47–52.

Gottman, J. M., & Levenson, R. W. (1988). The social psychophysiology of marriage. In P. Noller & M. A. Fitzpatrick (Eds.), *Perspectives on marital interaction* (pp. 182–200). Clevedon, England: Multilingual Matters Ltd.

Greenberg, L. S., & Johnson, S. M. (1986). *Emotionally focused couples therapy: An integrated affective systems approach.* In N. S. Jacobson & A. S. Gurman (Eds.), *Clinical handbook of marital therapy* (pp. 253–276). New York: Guilford.

Greenberg, L. S., & Johnson, S. M. (1988). *Emotionally focused therapy for couples.* New York: Guilford.

Griffin, W. A. (1993). *Family therapy: Fundamentals of theory and practice.* New York: Brunner/Mazel.

Griffin, W., & Crane, D. R. (1986). Nonverbal reciprocity in nondistressed marital partners: An examination of base rate change. *Journal of Marital and Family Therapy, 12,* 301–309.

Gurman, A. S., Kniskern, D. P., & Pinsof, W. M. (1986). Research on the process and outcome of marital and family therapy. In A. E. Bergin & S. L. Garfield (Eds.), *Handbook of psychotherapy and behavior change* (3rd ed., pp. 565–626). New York: Wiley.

Hahlweg, K., & Markman, H. J. (1988). Effectiveness of behavioral marital therapy: Empirical status of behavioral techniques in preventing and alleviating marital distress. *Journal of Consulting and Clinical Psychology, 56*, 440–447.

Hahlweg, K., Schindler, L., Revenstorf, D., & Brengelmann, J. C. (1984). The Munich marital therapy study. In K. Hahlweg & N. S. Jacobson (Eds.), *Marital interaction: Analysis and modification* (pp. 3–26). New York: Guilford.

Harper, J. M., & Elliott, M. L. (1988). Can there be too much of a good thing?: The relationship between desired level of intimacy and marital adjustment. *The American Journal of Family Therapy, 16*, 351–360.

Hetherington, E. M. (1972). Effects of fathers' absence on personality development in adolescent daughters. *Developmental Psychology, 7*, 313–326.

Hetherington, E. M. (1991). Presidential address: Families, lies, and videotapes (Address given to the Society for Research in Adolescence, Atlanta, GA, 1990). *Journal of Research on Adolescence, 4*, 323–348.

Hetherington, E. M., Cox, M., & Cox, R. (1982). Effects of divorce on parents and children. In M. Lamb (Ed.), *Nontraditional families: Parenting and child development* (pp. 233–288). Hillsdale, NJ: Lawrence Erlbaum.

Hetherington, E. M., Cox, M., & Cox, R. (1985). Long-term effects of divorce and remarriage on the adjustment of children. *Journal of the American Academy of Child Psychiatry, 24*, 518–530.

Hetherington, E. M., Stanley-Hagan, M., & Anderson, E. R. (1989). Marital transitions: A child's perspective. *American Psychologist, 44*, 303–312.

Hill, M. S. (1992). The role of economic resources and remarriage in financial assistance for children of divorce. *Journal of Family Issues, 13*, 158–178.

Holtzworth-Munroe, A., & Jacobson, N. S. (1985). Causal attributions of married couples: When do they search for causes? What do they conclude when they do? *Journal of Personality and Social Psychology, 48*, 1398–1412.

Jacobson, N. S. (1991a). Behavioral versus insight-oriented marital therapy: Labels can be misleading. *Journal of Consulting and Clinical Psychology, 59*, 142–145.

Jacobson, N. S. (1991b). To be or not to be behavioral when working with couples: What does it mean? *Journal of Family Psychology, 4*, 436–445.

Jacobson, N. S. (1991c). Toward enhancing the efficacy of marital therapy and marital therapy research. *Journal of Family Psychology, 4*, 373–393.

Jacobson, N. S., & Addis, M. E. (1993). Research on couple therapy: What do we know? Where are we going? *Journal of Consulting and Clinical Psychology, 61*, 85–93.

Jacobson, N. S., Follette, W. C., & Pagel, M. (1986). Predicting who will benefit from behavioral marital therapy. *Journal of Consulting and Clinical Psychology, 54*, 518–522.

Jacobson, N. S., & Holtzworth-Munroe, A. (1986). Marital therapy: A social learning/cognitive perspective. In N. S. Jacobson & A. S. Gurman (Eds.), *Clinical handbook of marital therapy* (pp. 29–70). New York: Guilford.

Jacobson, N. S., & Margolin, G. (1979). *Marital therapy: Strategies based on social learning and behavior exchange principles.* New York: Brunner/Mazel.

James, P. S. (1991). Effects of a communication training component added to an emotionally focused couples therapy. *Journal of Marital and Family Therapy, 17*, 263–275.

Johnson, S. M., & Greenberg, L. S. (1985a). Differential effects of experiential and problem-solving interventions in resolving marital conflict. *Journal of Consulting and Clinical Psychology, 53*, 175–184.

Johnson, S. M., & Greenberg, L. S. (1985b). Emotionally focused couples therapy: An outcome study. *Journal of Marital and Family Therapy, 11*, 313–317.

Johnson, S. M., & Greenberg, L. S. (1991). There are more things in heaven and earth than are dreamed of in BMT: A response to Jacobson. *Journal of Family Psychology, 4*, 407–415.

Laosa, L. M. (1988). Ethnicity and single parenting in the United States. In E. M. Hetherington & J. D. Arasteh (Eds.), *Impact of divorce, single parenting, and stepparenting on children* (pp. 23–52). Hillsdale, NJ: Lawrence Erlbaum.

Larson, J. H., & Holman, T. B. (1994). Premarital predictors of marital quality and stability. *Family Relations, 43,* 228–237.

Levenson, R. W., & Gottman, J. M. (1985). Physiological and affective predictors of change in relationship satisfaction. *Journal of Personality and Social Psychology, 49,* 85–94.

Locke, H. J., & Wallace, K. M. (1959). Short marital-adjustment and prediction tests: Their reliability and validity. *Marriage and Family Living, 21,* 251–255.

Maclean, M. (1992). Background facts from country reports. In L. J. Weitzman & M. Maclean (Eds.), *Economic consequences of divorce: The international perspective* (pp. 345–356). New York: Oxford.

Maclean, M., & Wadsworth, M. (1988). The interests of children after parental divorce: A long-term perspective. *International Journal of Law and the Family, 2,* 155–66.

Maddens, K., & van Houtte, J. (1992). Child support in Belgium. In L. J. Weitzman & M. Maclean (Eds.), *Economic consequences of divorce: The international perspective* (pp. 195–204). New York: Oxford.

Markman, H. J. (1991). Constructive marital conflict is not an oxymoron. *Behavioral Assessment, 13,* 83–96.

Markman, H. J., & Kraft, S. (1989). Men and women in marriage: Dealing with gender differences in marital therapy. *The Behavior Therapist, 12,* 51–56.

McLanahan, S. (1992). Intergenerational consequences of divorce: The United States perspective. In L. J. Weitzman & M. Maclean (Eds.), *Economic consequences of divorce: The international perspective* (pp. 285–310). New York: Oxford.

Newcomer, S., & Udry, J. R. (1987). Parental marital status effects on adolescent sexual behavior. *Journal of Marriage and the Family, 49,* 235–240.

Newfield, N. A. (1985). *Predicting divorce at marital therapy intake: A discriminant analysis model.* Unpublished doctoral dissertation, Texas Tech University, Lubbock, TX.

Oggins, J., Veroff, J., & Leber, D. (1993). Perceptions of marital interaction among black and white newlyweds. *Journal of Personality and Social Psychology, 65,* 494–511.

O'Leary, K. D., & Beach, S. R. H. (1990). Marital therapy: A viable treatment for depression and marital discord. *The American Journal of Psychiatry, 47,* 183–186.

Rausch, H. L., Barry, W. A., Hertel, R. K., & Swain, M. A. (1974). *Communication, conflict, and marriage.* San Francisco: Jossey-Bass.

Ross, E. R., Baker, S. B., & Guerney, B. G. (1985). Effectiveness of relationship enhancement therapy versus therapist's preferred therapy. *The American Journal of Family Therapy, 13,* 11–21.

Rutter, M. (1980). Protective factors in children's responses to stress and disadvantage. In M. W. Kent & J. E. Rolf (Eds.), *Primary prevention of psychopathology: III. Promoting social competence and coping in children.* Hanover, NH: University Press of New England.

Schaap, C. (1984). A comparison of the interaction of distressed and nondistressed married couples in a laboratory situation: Literature survey, methodological issues, and an empirical investigation. In K. Hahlweg & N. S. Jacobson (Eds.), *Marital interaction: Analysis and modification* (pp. 133–158). New York: Guilford.

Snyder, D. K. (1981). *Manual for the Marital Satisfaction Inventory.* Los Angeles: Western Psychological Services.

Snyder, D. K., Wills, R. M., & Grady-Fletcher, A. (1991a). Long-term effectiveness of behavioral versus insight-oriented marital therapy: A 4-year follow-up study. *Journal of Consulting and Clinical Psychology, 59,* 138–141.

Snyder, D. K., Wills, R. M., & Grady-Fletcher, A. (1991b). Risks and challenges of long-term psychotherapy outcome research: Reply to Jacobson. *Journal of Consulting and Clinical Psychology, 59,* 146–149.

Sorenson, A. (1992). Estimating the economic consequences of separation and divorce: A cautionary tale from the United States. In L. J. Weitzman & M. Maclean (Eds.), *Economic consequences of divorce: The international perspective* (pp. 263–284). New York: Oxford.

Spanier, G. B. (1976). Measuring dyadic adjustment: New scales for assessing the quality of marriage and similar dyads. *Journal of Marriage and the Family, 38,* 15–28.

Spanier, G. B. (1985). Improve, refine, recast, expand, clarify—don't abandon. *Journal of Marriage and the Family, 47,* 1073–1074.

Thomson, E., & Colella, U. (1992). Cohabitation and marital stability: Quality or commitment? *Journal of Marriage and the Family, 54,* 259–267.

Tschann, J. M., Johnston, J. R., Kline, M., & Wallerstein, J. S. (1990). Conflict, loss, change and parent–child relationships: Predicting children's adjustment during divorce. *Journal of Divorce, 13*(3-4), 1–22.

Wallerstein, J. S. (1985). Children of divorce: Preliminary report of a ten-year follow-up of older children and adolescents. *Journal of the American Academy of Child Psychiatry, 24,* 545–553.

Wallerstein, J. S. (1986a). Child of divorce: An overview. *Behavioral Sciences and the Law, 4,* 105–118.

Wallerstein, J. S. (1986b). Women after divorce: Preliminary report from a ten-year follow-up. *American Journal of Orthopsychiatry, 56,* 65–77.

Wallerstein, J. S. (1987). Children of divorce: Report of a ten-year follow-up of early latency-age children. *American Journal of Orthopsychiatry, 57,* 199–211.

Wallerstein, J. S. (1987–1988). Children after divorce: Wounds that don't heal. *Perspectives in Psychiatric Care, 24,* 107–113.

Wallerstein, J. S. (1991). The long-term effects of divorce on children: A review. *Journal of the American Academy of Child and Adolescent Psychiatry, 30,* 349–360.

Wallerstein, J. S., & Corbin, S. B. (1989). Daughters of divorce: Report from a ten year follow-up. *American Journal of Orthopsychiatry, 59,* 593–604.

Wallerstein, J. S., Corbin, S. B., & Lewis, J. M. (1988). Children of divorce: A ten year study. In E. M. Hetherington & J. D. Arasteh (Eds.), *Impact of divorce, single parenting, and stepparenting on children* (pp. 197–214). Hillsdale, NJ: Lawrence Erlbaum.

Wallerstein, J. S., & Kelly, J. B. (1979). Children and divorce: A review. *Social Work, 24,* 468–475.

Weiss, R. L., & Cerreto, M. (1980). The Marital Status Inventory: Development of a measure of dissolution potential. *The American Journal of Family Therapy, 8,* 80–86.

Weitzman, L. J. (1985). *The divorce revolution: The unexpected social and economic consequences for women and children in America.* New York: Free Press.

White, L. K. (1990). Determinants of divorce: A review of research in the eighties. *Journal of Marriage and the Family, 52,* 904–912.

Williams, A. M. (1979). The quantity and quality of marital interaction related to marital satisfaction: A behavioral analysis. *Journal of Applied Behavior Analysis, 12,* 665–678.

Zill, N. (1983). *Divorce, marital conflict, and children's mental health: Research findings and policy recommendations* (Senate Hearing No. 98-195). Washington, DC: U.S. Government Printing Office.

Zuk, G. H. (1991). Is divorce a major trauma? *Journal of the American Academy of Child and Adolescent Psychiatry, 30,* 1022.

NAME INDEX

SUBJECT INDEX